ALSO BY DAVID GIFFELS

All the Way Home:
Building a Family in a Falling-Down House

Are We Not Men? We Are Devo!
(cowritten with Jade Dellinger)

Wheels of Fortune: The Story of Rubber in Akron
(cowritten with Steve Love)

THE
HARD WAY
ON
PURPOSE

ESSAYS AND DISPATCHES
FROM THE RUST BELT

DAVID GIFFELS

SCRIBNER
NEW YORK   LONDON   TORONTO   SYDNEY   NEW DELHI

Scribner
A Division of Simon & Schuster, Inc.
1230 Avenue of the Americas
New York, NY 10020

Copyright © 2014 by David Giffels

Frontispiece courtesy of photographer Billy Delfs

All rights reserved, including the right to reproduce this book or portions thereof in any form whatsoever. For information address Scribner Subsidiary Rights Department, 1230 Avenue of the Americas, New York, NY 10020.

First Scribner trade paperback edition March 2014

SCRIBNER and design are registered trademarks of The Gale Group, Inc., used under license by Simon & Schuster, Inc., the publisher of this work.

For information about special discounts for bulk purchases, please contact Simon & Schuster Special Sales at 1-866-506-1949 or business@simonandschuster.com.

The Simon & Schuster Speakers Bureau can bring authors to your live event. For more information or to book an event contact the Simon & Schuster Speakers Bureau at 1-866-248-3049 or visit our website at www.simonspeakers.com.

Interior design by Jill Putorti
Cover design by Rodrigo Corral
Cover photograph © Alan Schein/Getty Images
Spine photograph © Eky Studio/Shutterstock

Manufactured in the United States of America

10 9 8 7 6 5 4 3 2 1

Library of Congress Control Number: 2013032606

ISBN 978-1-4516-9274-7
ISBN 978-1-4516-9275-4 (ebook)

"The Lake Effect" was previously published in *Rust Belt Chic: The Cleveland Anthology*.

"Cutting the Mustard" and portions of "Battleground" are reprinted with permission from the *Akron Beacon Journal* and Ohio.com.

"Unreal Estates" will appear (in another form) in *The New Heartland: Looking for the American Dream* by Andrew Borowiec.

For John Puglia, who always ventured first
1964–2013

CONTENTS

THE
HARD WAY
ON
PURPOSE

PART ONE

THE HEART
OF THE HEART
OF IT ALL

IT'S PRACTICAL TO HOPE.

-STUDS TERKEL

THE CHOSEN ONES

On the very afternoon I write these words, the second planet is about to pass directly in front of the sun, an event called the Transit of Venus, which, in silhouette, looks (though it cannot be viewed without appropriate eye protection) like a pea passing in front of a Hollywood searchlight, a minor epic of the cosmos that occurs just once every 105 years, which seems like a very long time until you remind yourself that this is Venus and the sun we're talking about. And also tonight, June 5, 2012, LeBron James will play an ostensibly meaningful basketball play-off game with the word HEAT lettered across his torso. And he will lose.

Whenever I try to unravel the Homeric epic of LeBron James (humble beginnings; burden of expectation; killer biceps; purpose-driven departure; grand quest; home, home, home, home, home; daddy issues; failure of pride; etc.), I find myself invariably, involuntarily, incessantly tracing a line backward through personal chronology and geography (his and mine), and then conversely forward, toward the potential infinity of those same territories. And I'm still, every time, left wondering whether this is as important as I think it is, and then utterly convinced that it is.

LeBron James was born into an identity crisis. He came into the world on December 30, 1984, and not just *the* world, but *a* world, a very particular world, one that would make him irrevocably who he is, and one from which he will never be able to extract himself. He was born into Akron, Ohio, at exactly the moment the city was losing all sense of what it was about, all confidence, all antecedent. He was like Swee' Pea in the *Popeye* cartoons, crawling out of the womb, oblivious and innocent, onto an I-beam dangling from a wire, everything falling apart methodically and chaotically behind him.

Two years before his birth, the last-ever passenger tire was built in Akron by a man named Richard Mayo, who paused afterward to look into a newspaper camera, a sturdy man in a V-neck T-shirt, thirty years on the job, his gloved fist perched on his hip, the other against his forehead, hands unsure what to do with themselves. The furrowed brow, the narrowed eyes, the strain at the corners—this was a look shared by men across a vast and hard-to-harness region, one defined ultimately and elliptically by water, by the Great Lakes and the Wabash and Ohio and Mississippi Rivers, routes of entry and departure to and from cities where the certainty of old factories was sagging and imploding.

Until then, for as long as anyone in my city could remember, Akron had been known as "the rubber capital of the world." Like most manufacturing cities in the industrial Midwest, this was plenty enough identity, and the reputation carried far enough and wide enough for the people here not ever to feel obscure or irrelevant, and this reputation rested on a civic infrastructure that provided solidity and security. Akron was the birthplace and the center of the world's tire industry, the most singular and there-fore the most overtly significant supplier to Detroit's auto indus-try. Which, yes, represents a stature something akin to being the Ralph Malph of the American industrial belt, and also a civic iden-tity that requires being inordinately passionate about radial tires. (In defense: the profoundly intertwined, ultimately tragic histo-ries—personal and corporate—of the Ford and Firestone families would have sent Shakespeare positively apeshit.) Anyhow, what more did we need to know? All the major American tire company world headquarters were here. Much of the production. Virtually all the high-tech research and development. The headquarters of the international rubber workers' union.

Tire-building was the city's defining profession. Tens, maybe hundreds, of thousands had made a good living at it, generation after generation. And then, one afternoon in August 1982, suddenly and completely that was gone.

A few months before, a photography exhibit called *Factory Valleys* opened at the Akron Art Museum. It made the city uneasy. Three years prior, the museum had commissioned Lee Friedlander, one of the most significant photographers in America, to come to Akron and make pictures. Any subject of his choosing. *We must be important,* the city thought. *And lovely to see.* Friedlander set off and started shooting. Cracked, empty streetscapes. Forlorn factories. Bent fences. Skewed signs. Punch-clock workers in ragged routine. He went up to Cleveland and down to Canton and over to Pittsburgh and came back again and again, through the monochrome winter of 1979 and into 1980. A pattern revealed itself into a story, and it was a story of ourselves and one we didn't yet quite know, and that is the worst kind of story: the one about yourself that you ought to know but somebody else has to tell you. Friedlander finished his work, and when executives of the bank that had sponsored his commission saw the grimy, hardbitten blackand-white pictures, they said this was not what they'd expected. This is not what we look like. This is not how we ought to be seen. They paid him his money but never showed the pictures in their branches. While the museum exhibited its collection, the commissioned pieces went into storage, locked in the dark. The bankers never gave a reason, but who can ever put reason to identity?

Then that same summer, a new term popped up in the American lexicon: Rust Bowl. It derived from Dust Bowl, another time, another place, someone else's eyes, the grim matrons of Steinbeck and Dorothea Lange. Soon it was bent into Rust Belt, and then it stuck like a barb. The first known use of the term was in a politician's speech in 1982. Akron, because it was so closely tied to a single industry, one that was disappearing like an exhale in the quick of a Lake Erie winter, was feeling a sudden and profound loss of identity. The term Rust Belt was sucked hard into that void and there it would stay.

If you look at a socioeconomic map of the broad Rust Belt region, you find, unmistakably, Akron at the dead center, geographically and philosophically set squarely between the automotive and steel regions. The city was among the first to hit bottom.

As all this was taking hold, right in the middle of that city LeBron James pushed his first basketball up into the air.

I graduated high school that summer of 1982, the same high school James would attend, St. Vincent–St. Mary, home of the Fighting Irish. We had many of the same teachers, sang the same "high atop a hill in Akron" alma mater, idled in the same "learning resource center," departed through the same glass doors every afternoon into a city we both love, but one best described as "unbeautiful." In fact, James and I share a unique quirk in NBA history: both of us went directly from St. Vincent–St. Mary to the Cleveland Cavaliers. I was an entry-level ball boy. He was the first pick in the NBA draft. But still. We knew what that meant. We both grew up well aware that Cleveland bears the unfortunate distinction of having suffered longer than any other American sports city without a championship in any major league.

The last time it happened was the year I was born, 1964, when the Cleveland Browns won the NFL championship game, which is what it was called then—the NFL Championship Game—which is to say the term Super Bowl didn't even exist yet. A lifetime like this. That's what LeBron James and I and our people share. A lifetime, one might say, of loss, but we here recognize something much different, more nuanced, more full of shadows. A lifetime of hope.

And anyone who's done both—hoped and lost—knows that in many ways hoping is worse.

My professional basketball career was short and relatively uneventful. I served during the worst seasons in the history of the team, some of the worst times ever endured by any sports franchise, an epically bad spell of losing and bizarre management and shabby catering and forgotten players in a time when the NBA was not yet prime entertainment. Eventually, I was fired by Ted Stepien, who is generally considered the most profoundly inept team owner in the history of American professional sports. The highlight of my tenure was the day the Cavaliers' arena, the old Richfield Coliseum, played host to the NBA All-Star Game and I escorted Bob Hope from his courtside seat to the home locker room so he wouldn't have to use the public restroom, then stood guard while he did his Bob Hope business at the urinal. My grandmother was stone-cold starstruck when I told her of this.

My tenure was marked by long, mind-numbing nights of home-team loss after home-team loss—twenty-four games straight, which stood as the longest losing streak in NBA history until 2011, when it was surpassed by . . . wait for it . . . the Cleveland Cavaliers. Inside that hollow concrete arena, I came to recognize the peculiar nature of loyalty, the way a small core of people kept re-upping their season ticket packages for a team that you couldn't give away tickets for. (And I mean this literally. Part of my ball-boy compensation was two complimentary passes to every game, and most nights those sat in the box office, unclaimed.) I came to recognize true loyalty in the likes of Joe Tait, the meat-and-potatoes Cavaliers radio announcer, who, despite Stepien's attempt to unseat him, returned after Stepien flamed out, and then Tait remained in the announcer's chair until retiring in 2011.

And in Rick Hofacker, the de facto manager of the ball boys who got me my job and went on to become a foot doctor specifically so he could in some way continue to serve the team he loved, which he has done now for many years, basketball feet being rather like NASCAR tires. And in Andy Bell, the team's equipment manager, whom I would spot off at the fringes of TV shots for years after my employment ended, still doing his job, much of which involved rich men's laundry. I saw a sometimes inexplicable but undeniably charming core of support for something that wasn't easy to support or even understand, and I came to regard it not as charity or mere fandom but something more complex: a symbiotic relationship of need.

The Cleveland Cavaliers of my adolescence needed to be loved. And the people of my place and time needed something to love. The seeds of this understanding were sown as I sat on my bony, polyester-warm-up-clad teenage ass on the hard wooden floor watching the nonsense of sport yearning for relevance, World B. Free gunning rainbows from the corner.

Give us something to root for. We'll take anything.

As I grew into early adulthood and observed a larger pattern of hope and loss and hope and loss and hope and loss, and the concurrent resilience thereof, I came to a begrudging conclusion: neither of these things—hope and loss—can exist without the other, and yet at every turn it is necessary to believe that at some point one will ultimately conquer. And that will be our legacy.

Half a generation after I graduated from that drab, ungarnished school building near the decaying central industrial core, James entered as a freshman and began one of the most star-crossed careers in the history of American sports. As a youth-league player, he had found the group of people he knew he belonged with, a tight collective of schoolyard friends who called themselves the Fab Five and who made a vow to keep their team together into high school. By his junior year, James was on the cover of *Sports Illustrated*, under the audacious title "The Chosen One." After that, everything got weird, in a specifically parochial way. James, a local teenager, was also an international superstar, the most promising athlete in the world. He represented a bizarre divide between the hyperreal details of my own place—living two miles from my house, walking the same hallways I had, eating carhop hamburgers at Swensons Drive In, befriending my best friend's son—and the notion of external identity that had vexed and eluded my hometown since I'd first begun to explore it. We in Akron began measuring James's personal reputation against our civic reputation, and hungering for the ways those two notions were aligned.

Who was he? Who were we? Were we him? Was he us?

Could this be what we've been longing for lo these many years?

In 2002, James, then a junior, was named *Parade* magazine's high school basketball Player of the Year. I was working as a columnist at the local newspaper, the *Akron Beacon Journal*. Because the paper carried *Parade* on Sundays, the magazine arranged for us to host a small awards ceremony in a meeting room just down the hall from the newsroom. A number of us made our way to the gathering that afternoon, drawn by the curiosity of this growing phenomenon whose story had become part of our daily working lives.

I sat in the back, watching. James had requested that his teammates join him, and so this group of young men in sweatpants and letter jackets all growing into themselves—one the size of a fifth grader; another who would soon sign as an Ohio State defensive lineman—sat at his flank with the awkward politeness endemic to Catholic schoolboys.

James was young, still slender, uncomfortable speaking in front of the small gathering, but he did his best and thanked his teammates and coaches, and everything he said seemed careful and true, in the give-110-percent-it's-all-about-the-team sort of way. He has always seemed earnest in such settings (a certain hour-long ESPN special notwithstanding). He has improved at public speaking, certainly, but even then there was an inscrutable purity about him—can one be confidently humble?—which has always been central to his demeanor. That afternoon, he seemed like a young man being fitted for a tuxedo, trying on a shell that didn't seem natural yet, but one—like this national award—that he was willing to grow into.

LeBron James had become a wrinkle in our journalistic routine. Almost daily, one of us had to answer the phone call, or the e-mail, or the chance query in the grocery store—why do you give so much attention to a high school athlete when there are real problems in the world?

The growing reality, however, was that maybe he was the solution to one of those problems, the answer to the very real, legitimately grave question of postindustrial American cities. Who are we? What are we?

As the ceremony finished and James gathered up his warm-up jacket and his award, I lingered in the room because I wanted to congratulate him. And also to fulfill an instinct left over from my younger days in an NBA locker room. I was curious how tall he seemed up close. (A universal male instinct: literally to size up other males. Once, lingering outside a concert venue, my brother eased in among the autograph seekers surrounding R.E.M. drummer Bill Berry and surreptitiously placed the flat of his palm atop his own head, extending it levelly toward Berry's, shooting me a revelatory and excited glance: *I am taller than a rock star!*) As James neared the door, I reached out my hand, and he reached back with a palm the size of a palm leaf. We shook.

"Congratulations," I said.

He nodded awkwardly, avoiding eye contact. He was either just a kid or he was a burgeoning aloof celebrity. I couldn't answer which, but I believe it was the former.

"We went to the same high school," I said. "Or I went to the same high school. That you go to now. I went to St. V."

He smiled, but he didn't say anything. I'm sure all those he met, even at that early stage, were looking for some context, measuring themselves against him, as it were. His eyes drew him toward the exit.

And then, through the kind of fate that never, ever, ever, *ever* happens here, particularly with regard to sports, the woebegone Cleveland Cavaliers drew the first pick in the 2003 draft lottery and selected James, who emerged as a man in full, wearing a suit as white as ice, diamonds in his ears, to become the hero of a team that needed one deep down in its soul.

> *You're not the one who has to worry about everything.*
> *The boy said something but he couldnt understand him.*
> *What? he said.*
> *He looked up, his wet and grimy face. Yes I am, he said. I*
> *am the one.*
> —CORMAC MCCARTHY, *THE ROAD*

I have spent my whole life watching people leave. This is a defining characteristic of the generation of postindustrial Midwesterners who have stayed in their hometowns. At every stage of opportunity, at every life crossroads, friends and family members and enemies and old lovers and vaguely familiar barflies depart. Piles of demographic and sociological data chronicle this, the term *brain drain* serving as a sort of catamaran counterpart to Rust Belt. Akron's population peaked the decade I was born and has dramatically fallen every decade since—from 290,000 in 1960 to 199,000 in 2010. High school graduation, college graduation, career opportunity, layoff, coming of age, crisis of confidence, marriage, divorce—the conditioned, perhaps prescribed, response is to go somewhere else. They all leave. A conversational quirk exists among natives of this region: Whenever we hear people say they've moved here from somewhere else, we instinctively respond, "Why?"

And so those of us who have stayed through all of our versions of those same life moments have a perpetual reflex of self-explanation, a desperation of identity, an instinctive yearning toward legitimacy and a kind of pride that is a far piece from Chamber of Commerce jingoism. Something that allows us to coolly intone, "It's a Rust Belt thing. You wouldn't understand."

Look, we don't get to be cool very often. We take it where we can get it.

There may, then, be no professional athlete in the history of American sports more directly connected to the narrative of his or her hometown. Plenty have played for the home team, certainly, but James seemed actually fated to play for the home team, as though he was conceived of this time and place, concocted from the ash of ourselves by some higher power, which power predestined the arrangement of those lottery Ping-Pong balls, and which power, if you're going to play along with this sort of stoner logic, would (if ours is a benevolent God) also have to have known about "The Decision," thus implying that we need to understand why maybe that was a necessary turn of events. For *us*.

Once we began to believe we deserved him, we slowly began to recognize that we would also deserve whatever he became.

James grew up with a definition of loyalty much like the one I'd developed watching those shitty old wine-and-gold Cavs. He reveled in his closeness to his childhood friends, to the neighborhood barber, to those Swensons hamburgers. After turning pro, he got the Akron area code—330—tattooed in chunky script down his powerful right forearm: sense of place, writ large. He would repeatedly, in a way that only the true, ear-to-the-ground native understands, make a formal distinction between Akron and Cleveland, two places that stand shoulder to shoulder, thirty-five miles apart, and are entirely similar yet entirely something of themselves. (There's an old saying here: it's a half hour from Akron to Cleveland and two hours from Cleveland to Akron. [It's a Rust Belt thing. You wouldn't understand.]) We make this distinction in great part as a matter of identity, the way brothers and sisters choose to express their individual personalities, even within the family.

So it wasn't just that he was from here and identified overtly with being from here. It was the very notion of what that identification implies. Factory towns, places that make things, are defined by work. That should be obvious. But when that is the prime element of integrity, it insinuates into the pores the same way soot once did. Here, uniquely, we do things the hard way on purpose. We recognize a virtue and a necessary creativity in choosing to do things that way. I once heard Jack White—a native Detroiter; one of us—say that he preferred playing plastic guitars that didn't go into tune, that the challenge was inspiring. If the keyboard onstage needs to be two feet away for him to reach it, he moves it three feet away. The struggle becomes its own aesthetic.

And unto this place comes the most promising athlete in the world, and the most famous (and for us, the celebrity is vitally important), who, if you're going to do things the hard way, couldn't have asked for much better than the 2003 Cavaliers. Soon a cliché emerged, about James carrying the team "on those broad shoulders of his." And not just the team, but all of us.

It wasn't that LeBron James was the solution to our identity crisis. It was that he was its embodiment.

*   *   *

I was working in my office on a gray Sunday afternoon near the end of the spring semester, chilly gusts sweeping at the windowpanes. In the middle of a recession that had gutted the industry, I'd left my newspaper job and begun teaching at the University of Akron. There was an echo of commotion from out on the commons, and I rose from my chair and looked down to see a steady progression of people heading toward the basketball arena, one building over from the English department. I was finished for the day and gathered my things and decided to walk the long way back to my car, to see what was happening. As I approached, I saw a big satellite dish above a television truck and realized what I'd just walked into. LeBron James was being awarded the NBA's 2010 Most Valuable Player award, and he'd arranged for the presentation ceremony to be held at the University of Akron gym, where he'd played many of his high school games. The year before, he'd also been named league MVP and had brought this same event to St. Vincent–St. Mary.

I arrived at a loose yellow police tape, clattering in the breeze, cordoning off the traffic circle in front of the arena. A couple hundred people had gathered, awaiting James's emergence from the building, hoping for a glimpse, maybe a wave, a handshake, an autograph. He'd led the team, once again, through a stellar season, and now, with a play-off series against the Boston Celtics about to begin, the hope was growing into something like belief that finally, after all these decades, our championship was within reach. He could be the one to take us there. I looked at my watch. I decided to stay.

Soon his teammates, who'd been there at his insistence to share the award, began to emerge, waving and joking as they slipped into expensive automobiles, some with drivers, some alone. The coach, Mike Brown, jogged past in a golf shirt, wiggling his hand in a goofy wave. And then, we waited. A lull settled. The sky bruised over with clouds. A cold drizzle began. Every now and again, a figure would emerge, generating a moment's excitement before the realization that, no, it's not him. TV guy. Security. Crew. Nobody.

The crowd began to dwindle. I stayed. I wanted to see him, this person I identified with in unique and paradoxical ways. We, who have nothing and everything in common.

The rain picked up. I reached into my bag for a little pop-out umbrella, soon realizing I was surrounded mostly by Sunday-afternoon dorm students and strays, and that college students, as a rule, do not own umbrellas, and so I felt a little guilty but also a little superior beneath the flimsy comfort of this one. My guilt and my superiority both were soon relieved when a grunt in a hoodie insinuated himself underneath.

Time dragged along. A half hour. Forty-five minutes. An hour. More. A late-afternoon chill had set in. The crowd grew impatient, small jeers brewing with each false alarm. A car pulled up, slowing into an auxiliary driveway right in front of where I was standing, stopping near the entrance where the TV crews had been soldiering in and out like ants after an ice cream social. It was the sort of luxury car that appears not to be a real model, but a full-size toy, a prototype for a movie, a gleaming two-tone sedan, classic yet inscrutable lines, a capped silhouette at the wheel. It sat there for a long time, chrome exhaust breathing papal smoke.

And then, finally, he emerged, in dark glasses, flanked by two hard men shaped like telephone booths. He was dressed in a silvery suit and a robin's-egg shirt, hurrying toward the car in a now-steady rain. The first shout rang from the crowd:

"Go *Celtics*!"

I looked in the direction of the voice, wondering. You stood out in the cold drizzle? For more than an hour? Just to do that?

James didn't respond. One of the attendants popped the trunk and James slipped off his jacket and handed it to him. The man laid it out carefully, smoothing the cloth. James hurried around the corner of the car to the back door, raindrops spattering his sunglasses.

"*Ass*-hole!"

He disappeared behind the rain-streaked glass. The car pulled out and away.

The Decision. Yadda.

So I watch him now in these games that he plays for Miami and try to unravel the complexity of my response. Because he's someone who still—just as others who've moved from Ohio into distant spotlights—represents my hometown, I want him to succeed personally. But not ultimately. Choosing Miami was choosing to *not* do things the hard way anymore. If there was a betrayal, that was it.

I want him to succeed, that young man from the newspaper conference room, so full of promise, of promises, of the hardest promises. But I want him to wish he were succeeding for us, for the only people who will ever really understand this desire of his to be, more than anything else, an identity.

I have heard James criticized for being more interested in his "brand" than his athletic legacy. But that's missing the point. His basketball talent, his basketball legacy, is a means to something else, and it's something unique in the history of sports celebrity. It's a means to the journey back through his own narrative, to translate the code written literally and figuratively on himself.

* * *

The *not* winning is the better story, you see, just in the same way that hope is harder than loss.

I say this as someone who came of age, who came to an understanding, in a city no one else wanted. I explored abandoned buildings in the years I spent downtown while attending classes at the University of Akron. I watched pieces of that ruin be reclaimed, adapted, not desperately, but methodically, through a Calvinist instinct adapted into the genetic code by way of the repetition of a three-shift factory town.

I don't know if James ever understood exactly why we needed him, otherwise he wouldn't have left the way he did. But I do think he understood—even (and maybe especially) in those insults—*how* we needed him. And maybe that's why he left the way he did.

Three weeks before *The Decision*, the University of Akron announced that it was launching the country's first baccalaureate program in corrosion engineering, a program that would soon attract millions of dollars in federal grants, the money indicating the value of research on how to repair and preserve rusting bridges and buildings and military facilities. It was a natural and poetic fit; understanding rust in Akron is like understanding grass in Tullamore. The first students entered the program just as James was beginning his career in Miami, a place that couldn't be more different from his home.

The city that had first introduced America to the notion of a Rust Belt was now offering America's first bachelor's degree in the subject. We dubbed it the Rust Institute.

We own that shit, and no one can take it away from us.

He'll be back. I write these words now on the night that it finally happened: James, the Most Valuable Player, leading the Heat to a

decisive championship; I, having immediately turned off the television after the final buzzer, not wanting to watch a celebration
that feels bitter and wrong. I look at those words and I really
believe them—*he will come home*—but I know I need to qual-
ify this belief. You come from a misunderstood place and you
develop a habit of qualifying *everything*—and I realize "hope" is
the only way to do so, to ultimately believe that *that* is the force
that will conquer, and I curse myself for this, for the goddamned
hope of it all.

STONES

I sat under a tree one summer afternoon around the turn of the millennium, watching men dismantle a giant smokestack.

This may sound like an overtly symbolic pastime, a depressing one too, for a young man in a city whose industry had collapsed. And a tedious one as well, considering the way they were going about it.

They were high up on a custom-rigged scaffold, a functionally ingenious contraption in a place whose defining quality is functional ingenuity. The ceramic-block smokestack was equally impressive: round and tall, elegant and unconcerned, a decommissioned leftover from a Firestone tire factory, with the company name lettered down its side. In its day, it looked like this

F
I
R
E
S
T
O
N
E

with smoke and sometimes a long banner of flame rising out of its top.

The men had erected a platform that surrounded the spire so they could take it down methodically, course by course. Handwork. They were removing the intricate puzzle of blocks a piece at a time and loading them into a bucket, which was lowered to the ground, emptied, then hauled back up for another round.

I don't know why they didn't just whack the thing with a wrecking ball. Plenty of other stuff around here has been erased that way, including Firestone's main factory, many years before, which the guy from the wrecking company once told me was the toughest building he'd ever encountered. It took two years to demolish. Someone had, apparently, predicted permanence.

I was glad they didn't just smash this one down. It was a nice afternoon, and I was enjoying the show. I sat on a scrubby little hillside, an embankment that ended at the railroad tracks that used to serve this vast industrial campus, each warehouse with a loading bay at the rear that opened up to where the freight cars would stop to be filled with cargo. A train still passes by here every afternoon, but it doesn't stop anymore.

The smokestack and its dismantlers were off in the middle distance, along a row of eight buildings in various colors of brick— yellow and ocher and rust colored. This particular smokestack was in the dusty-yellow range. Such nuances were important. I'd grown up in an awkward, uncertain spell—after the factories had stopped working, but before most of the abandoned ones had been bulldozed or converted to some other use (every child of the Rust Belt has eaten a restaurant hamburger in a cloyingly authentic brick-and-exposed-ductwork dining room). Within this cityscape and within a new era, I'd come to identify each of my hometown's major industrial enclaves not by what they produced, but by the color of their often-empty buildings. Goodyear and its surrounding neighborhood was classic university redbrick. Goodrich was a dirtier oxblood. Firestone was a buff yellow.

If there was an equalizer, it was smoke. Those of us who live in old houses in the city know that anytime we open up a wall or ceiling for repair or renovation, we can expect a fine layer of lampblack, the old smokestack pollution that was a cost of doing business. The closer you get to the central city, the more prominent the dark patina—on brick walls, bridges, even trees. I grew up amid urban churches whose common façade was flat-black sandstone, and it was a long time before I understood that sandstone was not naturally black.

And so these tall spires were the defining architecture of my hometown, mostly by default, as Akron has never had much of a skyline and never had much occasion to define its architecture. The town was built up fast, in busy times, without the luxuries of deliberation. Like that round Firestone chimney, these stacks stood as towers across the sky, lettered with the company names:

G
E
N
E
R
A
L

    G
    O
    O
    D
    Y
    E
    A
    R

F
I
R
E
S
T
O
N
E

G
O
O
D
R
I
C
H

You could see them from anywhere. Through most of the twen-tieth century, smoke poured out, all day and all night—sometimes white, sometimes black, sometimes in between, describing a rich spectrum of grays that only places like this understand—and a smell, the sulfurous rank of production, that became the way people described the city itself. Anyone who's lived near a steel mill or a paper factory knows this cultural tic: to try to explain the place by its particular stink. Akron has a weird twist on this—in addition to tire factories, the central city also once housed the Quaker Oats empire, so natives of a certain age have to calculate a nostalgic compromise between toasted grain and burning rubber.

So to happen along one day as one of these chimneys was being dismantled was occasion to sit and watch.

*   *   *

Generations knew this part of the country as the region that built modern America. I'm of the first generation that never saw any of that. *Postindustrial* is a much more relevant term to me than any of the many words and phrases—the Industrial Heartland; the Steel Belt; Industrial Valley—that are used to describe this broad swath of the country that produced automobiles and glass and tires and steel and an aesthetic of work and, most important, a new middle class.

For my generation, *postindustrial* is a rangy and encompassing and provocative adjective: a genre of music, a manner of dress, a style of art, a sociological term, a well-worn neologism, the end of the American century, an entire lifestyle. Increasingly, it is a new American culture.

In its present context, *postindustrial* emerged first as an underground concept, in the early 1980s. From time to time, I'd run across stylish ectomorphs in the Cleveland record shops, wearing punctiliously shredded Einstürzende Neubauten T-shirts and Herman Munster boots and accessories made of duct tape and a general attitude of being darker and aloofer than me. They smoked clove cigarettes and seemed to be studying graphic design.

One of them was Trent Reznor, whom I knew of first as a member of a local synthpop band called the Exotic Birds, a favorite of pretty girls who went out dancing, and whose local legend was cemented, for better or for worse, when they were chosen to open for Culture Club at the Richfield Coliseum. Reznor came across even then as intense, brooding, and driven—as birds go, he was more raven than exotic. Soon, his would become a widely recognized persona, as he donned black leather and chain-link mesh, became the figurehead of Nine Inch Nails, and released his debut album, *Pretty Hate Machine*.

The first time I remember hearing the term *postindustrial* used in any kind of specific mainstream way was when Nine Inch Nails emerged into prominence. They were one of the main-stage bands on the first Lollapalooza festival, which made a tour stop at Blossom Music Center near Cleveland in August 1991. The show was sold-out, and by late afternoon the affably hip audience, encompassing the kind of nonexclusivity one finds at such events in Ohio, had been into pretty much every band equally: Butthole Surfers, the Rollins Band, Ice-T, and Body Count. But when Reznor took the stage to that harsh electronic backdrop, hundreds, maybe thousands, of rock fans rushed the pavilion, demolishing the crowd barriers, scaling the seats, a crush that brought a look of utter fear and helplessness to the faces of the overwhelmed ushers. I was caught in the middle of it, swept forward involuntarily. It was frightening and thrilling. Reznor almost immediately stage-dove onto one of his own keyboards, destroying it. I'd never seen anything like it, and I was directly aware, even as my body was crushed toward the stage, that this was a Beatles moment. It felt both spontaneous and defining.

The notion of postindustry had no negative connotation for me. I had no referent for the prefix. It seemed cool and groundbreaking and uniquely relevant to my surroundings in ways I was just beginning to recognize. I didn't then understand the losses encompassed by the *post* part, nor the sense of pride and security once encompassed by *industry*. I was aware of a void, of all the empty buildings and the general diaspora of people my age, the recent graduates and emergent climbers who'd hightailed it to more promising lands. But to me that void just felt like something to be filled. It felt like opportunity. And it felt as if it were exclusively my own.

*   *   *

In the 1980s and '90s, a mass exodus took place from the Rust Belt. This included alarming percentages of the region's native-born young people. In the 2010 census, a psychological threshold was passed, as Akron's census count fell to 199,000, meaning the population had recoiled all the way back to its 1910 level, a hundred-year low. Proportionally, this figure exactly mirrors Detroit's latest census revelation: in both cities, all the growth of the twentieth-century industrial boom has been erased.

Having never left, I often wonder two things.

First: why does everyone always talk about the 30 percent who have departed, instead of the 70 percent who have stayed?

And second: where did they all go?

I don't know the first answer. I do know the second.

Phoenix.

The same census-takers that haunt the industrial Midwest like decennial locusts report that the population of Phoenix has grown from 439,170 in 1960 to 1,445,632 in 2010. Metaphorically speaking, all 1 million of those new residents came directly from Ohio. I know many of them personally. They post Facebook photos of sunsets and the labels of craft beers I've never heard of, and they send obliquely condescending meteorological updates, leading me to wonder if "It's a dry heat" is truly a favorable replacement for "It's not so much the heat, it's the humidity."

Phoenix: where the sports team is called the Suns, not the Browns; where there seems to be an entirely safe and logical set of career opportunities; where golf, not bowling, is the measure of a man's leisure; and where people from here go to die as though dying in a place with winter would simply be too much to bear.

The Rust Belt is the burden of America, and I don't mean in the sense that the rest of the country has to shoulder us. I mean in the sense that the 70 percent of us who have stayed have endured and tested and defined the burden in a way that might provide insight for a country that, lately, might welcome our lessons. We know the weight. We understand hard times. We've been called "dying" but haven't died. We know a few things.

If you want to nutshell the story of the American Industrial Belt, it's an ongoing narrative of arrival and departure. We understand America by virtue of living in melting pots that never completely gelled, and we understand America by virtue of living in places people had to leave.

I have spent my whole life watching people leave, but that's only a matter of timing. In another era, Ohio was the first safe stop on the Underground Railroad, a promised land of sorts, as escaping slaves crossed the Ohio River at the state's southern border. Prior to that, it was the farthest edge of the western frontier, a final destination until it was tamed enough for America to continue its expansion. Later, it was the destination of hopeful Europeans, countless scores of them, arriving by ship to work in the factories of Cleveland and Akron and Toledo and Youngstown and, more broadly, Detroit and Buffalo and Bethlehem and Duluth. And of poor Appalachians, who made their way up the pre-interstates, leaving dead farmlands and tapped-out mines behind. And African-Americans from the deeper South, seeking the same opportunity.

Many of them settled and acquired newspaper subscriptions and self-propelled lawn mowers and street-improvement tax bills. Others took the quick cash of a season in the mills and moved on. In a good healthy lapse in the middle, a stability, the culture matured. The culture of hard work and bowling trophies and Blatz and Pontiacs became a linchpin of Americana. But the notion of this new middle-class lifestyle as "having arrived" was a falsehood.

Sometimes I wonder if some of these cities were too big for their own good, often cramped and underplanned and overreaching and configured in such a way that the smell was the defining characteristic only because there was no logistical way to avoid it. A few years ago, Youngstown mayor Jay Williams launched a campaign called "Youngstown 2010," a systematic plan to "right-size" his city, whose population plummeted from 167,000 in 1960 to 67,000 in 2010. The idea was to eliminate vacant houses and neighborhoods to compress the city's physical size and scope to reflect its current state. Not to be ashamed of the reduction, but to resolve it.

When the men finished their work that day, they'd left a massive visual pun. I doubt they did this on purpose, but I like to imagine they did. The smokestack was halfway down.

F
I
R
E

was gone. What remained was

S
T
O
N
E

I have one of those blocks now from that very chimney. It is impressively crafted, heavy firebrick, with a honeycomb of holes, seven and a half inches wide, with a slight curve to its glazed outer surface, the color of a dirty Labrador retriever. It is tapered, so that when one block was fitted to the next to the next, they would form the curvature that eventually became the giant cylinder.

Someone gave it to me, one of those men who'd put in decades at what old-timers call "the Firestone," the definite article implying a sort of deification. He'd scavenged a few of those man-made stones, and he offered one as a gift.

POPULAR STORIES FOR BOYS

Lord, I *lived* inside those books. And they were not books that, conventionally speaking, you would choose to live inside, were you choosing to live inside some books. You would choose smart, new volumes: coffee-table books on hibiscus or vintage Vespas, I think, or you would choose something well glossed and shrink-wrapped, written by someone unthreateningly attractive and slightly more clever than you, someone like, say, Elizabeth Gilbert or Calvin Trillin, with whom you could put up for a while, like a hiking partner on the Appalachian Trail. (Yes: you would choose Bill Bryson.) You would not choose those books I chose on rainy Sunday afternoons when my parents took us to the used-book store near downtown, a place with rows and rows of faded spines organized by arcane, sometimes confounding principles of subject. "Paperback Fiction" covered the entire canon of, well, fiction published in paperback. But certain themes were diced and distilled to microscopic specifics such as "Aviation/WWII History/ Allies/Lighter-Than-Air" and "Jewish Studies/Akron & Area." There were tantalizing subcategories of antique firearms but no hint anywhere of the corresponding violence and death that is the platonic craving of the American boy.

The store was in an old building one ring from the center of town, and during the drive there—tucked with two brothers and a sister into the backseat of a gray AMC Pacer—covering the four miles from our house near the edge of the city, I could sense the gentle downhill slope toward downtown. If you ran out of gas and were in no hurry, you could roll there.

Industrial cities almost invariably evolved outward from their lakes and rivers, guided by liquid muses. Akron originally evolved as a canal town—the main drag once made of water—and later as a factory town, and so its development was based more on the principles of gravity and flow than the engineered order of lines and grids. The center of town was low, where the canal found its easiest course, and the neighborhoods evolved up the gentle slopes according to the prevailing winds. The poorest people lived in the places that smelled the worst and where settled the highest concentrations of soot, and the ascending classes followed in order, so that the castles (and some were *actual* castles) built by the wealthy founders and company presidents were just beyond reach of their own by-products of smoke and ash. Don't shit where you eat, the saying goes.

From where we parked for the bookstore, I could see the tall, round smokestacks of the B.F. Goodrich complex just yonder, and beyond that the tall, round smokestacks of Firestone. Viewed from this vantage, the spiked architecture of the smokestacks collectively formed a sort of bar code against the sky, as if they composed the imprint of our true self. Even on a Sunday, the air hung with a burnt pungency of sulfur, which I inhaled with equal shares of attraction and repulsion. It was like that glass jar of gumdrops on your grandmother's table: maybe sweet and maybe spice.

Inside the store was a cat that lay across the counter, obvious as a stage prop, watching us wander into our places. The owner, Frank Klein, was built with the sturdy earthiness of a russet potato—thick fingers and brawny shoulders and rocky facial features studded with sharp blue eyes. He looked like a relief map of Maine. His hair and beard were of the same shape and consistency as that on my Kung-Fu Grip G.I. Joe, whose follicles were described in the packaging as "lifelike." Mr. Klein was highly social and often engaged my parents, and sometimes me, as we moved past the cat and into the store.

The store was called the Bookseller, the pun of whose name I had figured out myself at an earlier age when entendre represents revelation—*seller . . . cellar!*—and which I still appreciated as I headed toward the downstairs. The basement, underlit, musty, and damp, was devoted to books that a book dealer wouldn't feel uncomfortable storing in such a place, and that's where I always headed because that's where I had previously discovered a green volume whose glue had turned to the prediluvian dust of saints' bones, a book whose title—*Popular Stories for Boys*—was rendered entirely ironic by time, as it was published in—well, I don't know what year because the unhinged spine had released the title pages and the first two pages of text. Suffice to say that the "boys" with whom this book may originally have been "popular" had likely read it by gaslight, in shirtsleeves and suspenders. Because of the missing pages, I started on page three, halfway through a word that soldiered on without the aid of its lost prefix:

. . . truding from the body. But there was no sign of this—only a tiny hole through the center of its forehead, from which blood was oozing.

I was hooked.

Popular Stories for Boys compiled four complete books: *Bomba the Jungle Boy*; *Sky Riders of the Atlantic*; *Bob Dexter, Club House Mystery*; and *Wrecked on Cannibal Island*. It ran on close to nine hundred pages and I read them all. This book, and those that followed, did many things for me in terms of imagination and aesthetic and the rituals of reading and so on. But first, mostly, and most profoundly, they took me down with their smell.

As if in response to the olfactory challenge of the factory-town air, the books in that basement were pungent and complex—dust, pulp, ink, cotton duck, binding strings—and when I found myself alone, I pulled down a volume and buried my nose into the center crease, pulling the sage up into my nostrils until I needed to exhale and inhale again. Sometimes (first looking this way and that) I touched my tongue to the page for a taste.

Here was an invocation: however deeply I could draw the scent into myself—literal inspiration—I could then exhale my wish for the answers to all these sacred mysteries.

From the time I learned to read I knew that I wanted to be a writer, and I knew exactly what that meant: I had committed myself to an insoluble mystery. I had no idea how books were made, nor any manifestation of who made them. Half the time, the name of the person on the cover turned out to be a pseudonym, fictions within fictions—Samuel Clemens mingling with Poor Richard and Theodor Geisel and for God's sake Theo. LeSieg—all of them pouring stories through their funnels of deception.

Following the direction of *Popular Stories for Boys*, I took particular interest in books on the subjects of the American past, but more specifically, I sought books written *in* the American past, so that my childhood library and the vocabulary I absorbed by osmosis was markedly anachronistic, with titles such as Arthur M. Winfield's *Rover Boys Out West* from the "Rover Boys Series for Young Americans," published in 1900 by the Mershon Company (a used book, inscribed "For Byron in the hope he may enjoy reading about the Rover Boys Out West," and signed "Uncle Bob, May 14, 1932," an inscription that seemed oddly redundant).

I also read Winfield's *Poor but Plucky* from the "Bright and Bold" series and some of the Jerry Todd books he wrote: *Jerry Todd and the Purring Egg*, *Jerry Todd and the Whispering Cave*, etc. (The prolific Arthur M. Winfield turned out to be the pen name of a man known to the civilian world as Edward Strate-meyer. Mysteries within mysteries.)

I read *The X Bar X Boys at Nugget Camp* (1928) and *The X Bar X Boys in Thunder Canyon* (1926), installments in a series by James Cody Ferris, which if that was his real name is awesome.

All these books had certain elements in common. They began with fanciful frontispieces, black-and-white illustrations captioned with a snippet of text:

In her hand the woman held a long barreled rifle.

Walter sprang in to save the lives of the horses.

Bomba brought the paddle down with all his force.

Nearly every chapter ended with a cliff-hanger, which often literally included someone hanging off a cliff.

Yes, sir, the Cap'n had been knocked out by a loaded catchup bottle. And the mysterious humpback who had committed the deed had escaped into the night.

Eventually, I recognized that many of these books were published by Grosset & Dunlap. I can't say that I went specifically looking for that imprint on the spine, but by early adolescence, I could be best described as a "G&D man." I carried the belief that "pluck" was among the most desirable personality traits a young man could possess, and also that it was not unusual for boys to drink black coffee nor to whittle as a pastime, nor to have friends named Red and Stumpy and Slim and High Hat Frank (a tramp, an actual tramp!) nor also to be heroic orphans. I called skunks *polecats* and knew that when the time came to put my acquired knowledge into practice, I would be able to identify fool's gold by pressing it between my teeth.

I also believed that normal human conversation was conducted in highly expository back-and-forth exchanges of quick wit and hyperbolic dialect:

"And what do you think about it, Pop?" Roy asked at length. "Any pronounced opinions on the subject?"

"You mean about goin'?"

"I mean about the chances of striking gold at Nugget Camp."

"Oh!" The old puncher rubbed his chin thoughtfully. "Well, if you really want to know, Roy—I think the chances are pretty blame good!"

These books led to an interest in fanciful history (*The Life of Kit Carson, The Oregon Trail, With Crockett and Bowie: Fighting for the Lone Star Flag*), and then led sort of accidentally to *Narrative of the Life of Frederick Douglass: An American Slave*, and then by calculated chance to Laura Ingalls Wilder. I may be the only heterosexual boy in Ohio history who not only read all the *Little House* books, but also as a result took up sewing because the skill seemed absolutely necessary to my survival here on the lone prairie. (Which was actually the twin bed in the room I shared with my late-twentieth-century, middle-class brother.)

These books, most of them, shared one other common trait. In their opening pages, on that thick cottony paper, were lists of other titles. By 1927, for instance, Arthur M. Winfield had written a "first" Rover Boys series consisting of twenty titles, and a "second" series of ten more, and also, apparently in his downtime, six titles of a Putnam Hall series, which I'd never even seen. This list wasn't complete. It didn't mention Winfield's Bright and Bold series, published in the late nineteenth century, a series at whose scope and breadth I could only guess, because the list on the *Poor but Plucky* title page indexed a few titles followed by "etc., etc.," suggesting that Mr. Winfield's prolificness was best not expressed in finite terms.

Leo Edwards, meanwhile, had already published eleven books in the Jerry Todd series, plus eight Poppy Ott books, three Trigger Berg books, and four Tuffy Beans. (A previous owner of this copy of *Jerry Todd and the Purring Egg* had penciled marks next to the titles—check marks and little circles, apparently to indicate those read and those yet to be read, an accounting of desire whose echo carries into the Amazon Wish List.)

The bit of copy that preceded the list indicated a body of work filled with "Pirates! Mystery! Detectives! Adventure! Ghosts! Buried Treasure! Achievement!"

The list of books in the X Bar X Boys series ended with a preemptive strike: "Other volumes in preparation."

Books were being written everywhere, at every hour of the day and night, in the mystery of creation, but with such speed and efficiency that they could not be accounted for by anything but the promise that they would come, they would come, they would come. Mystery! Adventure! Buried Treasure! Achievement! Etc.!

All of this combined to make two things quite clear, both of which were ultimately depressing.

1. I would never be able to read all the books.

2. If I wanted to be a writer, I was already dreadfully far behind.

The idea of choices was complicated in the industrial Midwest.

It wasn't just that this was a land of plenty. It specifically was a land of plenty for a newly mature and uniquely American set of consumers, a deeply nuanced middle class that begged for equally nuanced ways to indulge its proud discretionary income. The suburban shopping mall had almost completely replaced the urban downtown department store, and its concoursed nooks and honeycombs catered to increasingly concise stratifications of patronage. (Think a Chess King man would be caught dead in a Frye boots outlet? Think again, hombre.) Mail order found its sweet spot in the era between the Sears Wish Book and the Internet. We received catalogs in our mailbox by the rubber-banded bundle: Lands' End, Sharper Image, Renovator's Supply, Best Products, and on and on.

K-Mart, meanwhile, as the proletarian standard-bearer, was deepening its sensitivity to its own micro-demographics and would soon, depending on the locale, evolve into Super K, Big K, K-Mart Super Center.

The first two K-Mart Super Centers were built in suburbs of Akron. We were the national test market, and we embraced that like an honor. In the same way that Ohio seems invisible and irrelevant to the rest of the country until it comes time to elect a president, so too is it the kind of place whose clientele might seem nondescript until it comes time to put a mainstream, middle-class, mass-market shopping concept through its paces. Then a little eureka-bulb lights up.

Ohio!

As a rookie small-town newspaper reporter in 1991, I covered the opening of the very first K-Mart Super Center in the suburban town of Medina, Ohio. It was a huge event locally, with a ribbon cutting and throngs of curiosity seekers, and it also drew national media coverage. The news of the day included a woman's wandering through the parking lot, crying and lost, unable to find her car in the vast acreage of automobiles. The police finally got involved, and after an extensive search the two were reunited.

My dad, a civil engineer, designed the parking lot for the second location, and I'd like to think that my Sunday-dinner consultations with him helped stave off another such misfortune.

I'm sure the K-Mart corporation chose industrial Ohio to launch this concept based on the area's public perception as quintessentially *working class*. But in places such as Akron and Cleveland and Detroit and Milwaukee and Pittsburgh, we understood that term with a different nuance than its usual usage, in which *working class* implies the next tier down from *middle class*, and probably a couple of tiers down from *white collar*. Here, the working class had for decades been the most stable, most prosperous, most highly regarded local demographic. In Akron, tire builders referred to themselves as the "kings" of the rubber industry, without irony. They were highly paid, backed by an extraordinarily powerful labor union, and thanks to years and years of hard-nosed contract negotiations, they enjoyed exceptional job security and benefits. In Akron, the working-class families were the ones with the Cadillacs and the vacation homes and the high-end kitchen makeovers. My dad had a college degree and was a partner in a small engineering firm. Yet people like him—small-business owners, nonunion professionals—were far more susceptible to the swings of the economy and didn't have the same clout as the factory workers. My dad wore a suit to work, but he'd never owned a new car.

Before K-Mart's cultural revolution, smaller regional chains were more likely to cater to that middle class of consumers with a sort of midsize mom-and-pop style. In the region around Ohio, the Gold Circle discount stores established themselves as a dominant consumer force in the 1970s and '80s. Gold Circle could be compared to K-Mart on something like a three-quarters scale, but it carried itself with the distinctly bourgeois personality that comes from marketing mass culture to a willing middle class, an up/downscale suggestion that quality is necessary, but only so much and then it becomes a liability; this same philosophy was employed to great effect by Timex watches and the Steve Miller Band.

Gold Circle was the first chain of stores to use bar codes on all its merchandise, a mark of facelessness in the name of efficiency that seemed particularly well tuned to people who worked on assembly lines. It seems no coincidence that the very first commercial scan of a UPC label took place here, in an Ohio grocery store, in 1974, just about exactly the moment our identity was spiraling into oblivion.

My parents loved Gold Circle because it carried a broad

range of merchandise that approximated the A-list offerings of suburban-shopping-mall department stores, but at a considerably lower price. As a result, I had a pair of sneakers that looked to my parents exactly like the supercool Adidas Country running shoes (white leather; green stripes, suede yokes on the heel and the toe) that I not only coveted, but needed if I was ever going to achieve any level of cultural relevancy. My Gold Circle sneakers were indeed white running shoes, and unabashed knockoffs of the Adidas Country, but they were made not of leather but of a substandard polyvinyl that cracked prematurely, and worse, they had not three, but *four* stripes down the side. I may as well have shown up to gym class with an extra leg.

In an era when a down-filled ski jacket was a very particular status symbol (pretty people skied), I had a Gold Circle coat that was clearly a cheap approximation—not puffy and robust as in the resort photographs, but instead insulated with stitched rows of flimsy polyester batting. I was therefore marked by my garment as the industrial-Midwest version of an upper-subcaste dalit.

The winters were long and harsh, and I actively avoided going outside in that coat. So I holed up with my books instead. Even this attempt at dignity and freedom was complicated by my parents' having found, at Gold Circle, sets of Bancroft Classics, abridged versions of the Western canon. These books came in boxed literary six-packs, like those beers of the world, where you like four of them very much and tolerate the rest simply because they're beer. So I'd get a set that included *Around the World in 80 Days* and *Kidnapped* and *Robinson Crusoe* and *The Man in the Iron Mask*, but also included *Heidi* and *Great Expectations*.

I read them all and then others too. I read *The Lone Ranger and the Mystery Ranch* lying on my bed inside a sleeping bag one Christmas break. I have never been more comfortable. I read

Where the Red Fern Grows propped in the limbs of a backyard apple tree. I have never been more uncomfortable.

I read in sunbeams and in a hammock and stretched out under the dining room table and in an old, exceedingly ugly swivel chair that smelled like dog.

I'll never know if I was a natural introvert, or if I had simply found something preferable and contrary to public life: the secret confidence of Grosset & Dunlap.

The bookstore was on fire.

I suppose I smelled it first, though that's hard to say. The fire's announcement came whispering to almost every sense before it revealed itself whole. It got to my nose before I'd stepped into my car, nearly a mile away, but I thought little of that, preoccupied as I was with the end of the first day of my first serious job, writing for the local newspaper, the *Akron Beacon Journal*. Even if I'd taken greater notice, it likely wouldn't have raised concern. Even then, 1994, long after the factories had closed, the smell of smoke remained part of the olfactory personality of the central city.

Starting toward home, I felt the splash of one of the narrow rivers winnowing downhill as it sprayed up into my wheel wells, but paid it little heed. I heard the cavalry of sirens and the heavy engines urging through their gears. Then, as I crested the old canalway and climbed the hill up from downtown, I saw a wreck of smoke twisting into the sky. The closer I got, the more it drew me from my preoccupation with the day's events. The question grew: What's burning? And soon, with quickly decreasing possibilities, the answer.

By the time I reached the makeshift detour, I knew. In ugly orange flames drenched in black, the question fell away. The Bookseller was raging, full on. The bookstore where I'd spent all those childhood Sunday afternoons was burning down. On the first day of my real writing life, the place that had made me want to be a writer was disintegrating before my eyes. If it weren't so tragic and true, the irony would have been too cheap even for a Jerry Todd melodrama.

There were firefighters everywhere, dozens of them, and trucks parked this way and that. The sidewalks were packed with onlookers. A water cannon was blasting at the building, and spray came from two aerial ladders angled above the roof. Water was gushing out the front door.

But nothing could stop it. I knew that, even as I idled in the slowed traffic, the line of us gawking as we waited for our turn into the detour. Some of them might have thought, with all those trucks and all those hoses, that the firefighters had a chance. Not me. Because I knew what fueled the flames: cottony, ink-drinking pages nestled in dried bindings, duck and string, bonded by old glue that cracked against its reopening. Volumes upon volumes upon volumes, tens of thousands of them, their infinite letters the tinder of a conflagration that nothing could extinguish.

It was a monstrous thing to see, savage and insurgent. Although the old bookstore was the first place to teach me the existence of every possibility, of every hope, I knew nothing could stop this. And it was true. The building was a complete loss. Countless books, most of them rare and collectible, were destroyed. Frank Klein, still running the business, was sixty-eight years old. It seemed as if it had to be the end.

But it wasn't.

Mr. Klein salvaged what he could, found another old building, and set up shop again. As I write this nearly twenty years later, he's still running the business, still going into his shop every day, still tending to something he understands better than anyone else could. I go to see him from time to time, and he always greets me

warmly, asks about my parents, remembers something I was interested in years before. Every once in a while, he sets something
aside for me, thinking I might be interested.

I doubt he knows how much he and his store meant to me as
a child, and I doubt he knows what it means to me now as an
example of something that seems so true about this place, the
part of *working class* that says maybe the struggle is the only true
freedom.

DELTA LOWS

This was not the world that had put us to bed. This was not a world we'd seen anywhere, not in the moon shots nor the *Scholastic News*, not in the downtown department-store-window wonderlands nor the collected works of Rankin/Bass. This was snow, yes, and January snow along the Great Lakes was as obvious as the nipple in Farrah Fawcett's swimsuit. But not like this.

We'd gone to bed, my brother, Ralph, and I, in our shared attic bedroom, with the temperature mild, above freezing, and no expectation of a storm. And now we'd awoken to the sound of a winter hurricane, a sound that reached down our throats and gripped hard on our hearts, the other hand grabbing us by the nutsacks, a sound running its outlaw flag up our spines, and we peered out the frosted windows at our known universe, and we could not recognize a thing. The snow had not just fallen deep—twelve new inches on top of the sixteen inches already on the ground—but was being driven asunder by a terrifying anarchic wind, whipped into peaks where flatness should be, scooping out its own road in defiance of the taxpayers' pavement, piling a sharp, white dune against the neighbor's parked car, shaping shrubs into rain barrels and rag mops and hippopotami.

We leaned obliquely over the radiator, side by side, looking out the twin set of windows, their panes frosted with the difference between the escaped steam and the irrational weather outside.

We gazed into the predawn at something terrifying and beautiful, neither of which adjective applied well to the city we knew. Akron was many things, most of them good (though fewer by the year), but drama was not its forte. It was steady and safe, a place where every twentieth-century generation until our own could bank on a lifetime job with one of the rubber companies. What we saw was everything we knew suddenly turned completely foreign, and it did not feel good. We didn't then know the meteorology of what was happening—that the temperature had just dropped from thirty-four to thirteen between 5:00 and 6:00 a.m.—twenty-one degrees in less than an hour—that the barometer had plummeted to 28.28 inches, the lowest reading ever recorded in the United States outside the tropics; that the winds were gusting over one hundred miles an hour, that the windchill was sixty below. We did not know we were in a winter hurricane. We did not know a trucker had become buried in a giant snowdrift on the highway and would survive the next six days eating snow, a long tube stuck out the window for air. We did not know of roofs torn off and windows imploded, of trees toppled and a helicopter bouncing across the airport grounds like a paper crane. We just knew what we heard: a high, freakish howling like nothing we'd ever before heard. And it was that—not the wind itself, but the *sound* of the wind—that drove through the thin gaps of the inefficient, old sashes and touched us like a bad fiction of the undead.

In the predawn, we saw plummeting flakes big as Communion hosts. The snow in the air and on the ground turned in drunken, violent swirls. Everything familiar was obliterated.

I loved to read stories about scenes like this, about homesteaders on the prairie tunneling their way from the kitchen to the barn, snow piled to the second-story windows, and the harrowing dialogue of escape that unfolded over harsh, hot coffee back safe at the kitchen stove. *Joe. They called their coffee joe.* About soldiers on the Western Front tracking red trails across cold, nihilistic snowscapes that would darken the rest of their lives. About cowboys stranded on the high plains melting snow to keep them alive, capable men of the land who knew that eating it cold would spell their end.

One other thing we did not yet know: that sophisticated people consider *talking about the weather* code for boring conversation. We didn't know this because in Ohio most days, the weather is the most dynamic and remarkable aspect of our existence. Daily, it lays waste to our plans, it depresses us, it makes us laugh and marvel. It has its own language and legend. We speak of the *lake effect* and the *snowbelt* and *Delta lows* and *Alberta clippers*, of a lascivious summer humidity and a winter cold that cracks us like eggs. We pass down legends of the 1913 Flood, the '88 Drought, and, more than anything else, this: the Blizzard of '78, for which the phrase *storm of the century* is statistical fact.

Weather, in places like this, *is* culture.

I fumbled for my glasses in the dark, finding them on top of my dad's old footlocker at the end of my bed, a big metal trunk whose army-drab top I'd covered in Wacky Packages stickers. We went downstairs.

An empty juice glass with a bit of grapefruit pulp in its bottom indicated my father was already up and gone. Gone, despite the day. He'd left a note. He'd set off on foot with a shovel for his office a mile away. My dad was a partner in a small civil-engineering firm, the kind of place that in Akron in those years relied almost completely on work from the tire companies, as did virtually all of the city. That source was crumbling at every corner, and my dad must have felt that he couldn't take a day off, even a day like this, for fear of losing more. So he was off shoveling snow that was being blown haphazard by fifty-mile-an-hour gusts, which is like trying to line up cocaine-injected lab rats single file for inspection. But that is the nature of this place—and it is the nature of my father, and, I think, of all the men of this place—to *do*, for the sake of doing. We are restless to begin with, and we are of a place that does not look kindly on rest. So my father shovels snow that will not stop moving and says he is doing it because it needs to be shoveled.

Thus we will do the same. Ralph and I will pull on every layer we can manage, tube socks covered by baseball stockings covered by our father's old woolen army socks covered by plastic baggies covered by green, steel-shank rubber boots. Long johns and sweatshirts and flannel and tragic polyester ski jackets. And then we will take up shovels from the garage.

Every family in the American Midwest has a collection of shovels accumulated across generations and ranked by hierarchy. The term *good shovel* has the same meaning and relevance in this region as *good shoes* has in the Bible Belt. Ralph, being the alpha male, would lay claim to our grandfather's wooden-handled, wide-bladed plow shovel—the "good shovel"; I would be relegated to a contemporary plastic thing with a flat blade—the "chump shovel." And so we would begin.

I am descended from engineers. Tinkerers and builders and puzzlers; men who sometimes invented problems just to solve them. My grandfather, for instance, built his own table saw. It takes an Escher-like hybrid of pragmatism and imagination to build a table saw when you have no table saw with which to build it. You wonder where a mind gets to thinking that way.

I knew that my grandfather had served in World War I, but that's about all I knew of the subject. I knew there were awards and medals, but not how they had been earned. I knew the clothing I'd secretly tried on in his attic—a woolen overcoat; a leather belt—while a half dozen uncles drank beer and howled down-stairs, a laughter of sheer force. But I knew nothing of where or how or why these things had been worn. I didn't know the things I really wanted to know: whether he had fired a real gun, if he had jumped into a dark foxhole only to find himself face-to-face with an enemy soldier; if he had gone through the pockets of a dead man to find the picture of his wife and child. Which is to say that I could only understand my grandfather's service by imagining him through the prism of *All Quiet on the Western Front*, which I had found on my parents' bookshelves and read one summer in the limbs of the backyard apple tree. Which is to say I knew nothing of life, not even the lives directly surround-ing me.

Only many years later, long after his death, did I learn he had been part of a little-known mission that no one, not even those who took part, ever quite understood. I found, among the boxes that represent the luggage of my lifetime, a booklet of poems writ-ten by a man named R. S. Clark and titled *The Creation of Russia*. I'm not sure how it got in with the rest of my books, but it was tucked between volumes I'd kept as mementos of my grandpa: an indigo hardback titled *Geologic Survey of Ohio* and a brown one called *Roofs and Bridges: Stresses*. Inside the cover of the slim poetry collection was a handwritten note, dated 1958, from one of the men he'd served (and no doubt suffered) with. One would expect this sort of note of such men who came from a place and time when hardship was held inside until it passed, like a gallstone, ruggedly and without remark, men from the Corps of Engineers:

Apparently Rodgers had these printed some time in the past. They are sent with the compliments of his son Dick.

*   *   *

On September 4, 1918, just as the war was nearing its end, fifty-five hundred befuddled American soldiers found themselves crunching their mittened hands under their armpits for warmth and stamping their feet against the frozen ground of Archangel, a little town in northern Russia. The air was frigid and a cold sun lay low on the horizon. The goddamned army had issued them boots with slick, treadless soles, footwear better suited to a fight-or-flight-can't-get-any-traction nightmare than battle maneuvers in the snow and ice. Most of the soldiers, including my grandfather, were from Michigan, men in their twenties who'd received penny postcards instructing them to report to Fort Custer in Battle Creek. In the fruitless poetry of operations, they were called the American North Russian Expeditionary Forces. Around carefully shielded campfires, they renamed themselves the Polar Bears.

My grandfather, an army engineer, lived in a boxcar where he and his fellow infantrymen puzzled over how to face an enemy that wasn't exactly an enemy in a battle that wasn't part of a war. Even if that question had an answer, it wouldn't have done any good. Illogic was the only certainty to their time in the far north. On Armistice Day, November 11, as the rest of the human race recognized the end of the Great War, the Polar Bears—the 339th US Infantry—were in a battle with thousands of raging Bolsheviks, a fight that was as gruesome as it was ambiguous. The war was over, yet the close combat went on for four days, with twenty-eight Polar Bears killed and seventy wounded, and more than five hundred Russian casualties.

So isolated were the soldiers that they could only guess at why they were fighting or what might be happening back home, so far away. They were caught in the middle of another nation's revolution, dispatched to fight the *idea* of something, which always makes for a difficult motivation, especially where homicide is concerned. They didn't know that a letter-writing campaign was under way, calling for the nation's leaders to bring them home. They didn't know that President Woodrow Wilson was harboring private regret for his decision to send them there, admitting later, "I have at no time felt confident in my own judgment about it." They were sick and freezing, ill equipped, wondering if they'd been chosen only because they were natives of the snowy upper Midwest, and whether anyone had any idea that it was *never* this cold back home. They pulled boots off dead Bolsheviks and put them on their own feet, throwing away the useless ones issued by their own military.

The Creation of Russia is mostly about two things: cold and the question why. It opens with a poem called "Memorial Day Prayer," filled with a particular kind of hurt, first for "thy children who have died," but more for the injustice of being sent to kill and die without a mission, its final line pleading, "Oh, make our duty plain."

By midwinter, the issue of whether they should be transported home was irrelevant. The Russian ports were frozen and there was no way out. So the fighting went on, the Americans firing unreliable, Russian-made Mosin-Nagant rifles and Lewis machine guns into relentless waves of Russian soldiers, whose attacks continued through the winter and into the spring.

One soldier wrote of their plight in a letter home: "We had to fight to save our necks and that's what we did. We didn't know why we were fighting the Bolsheviks. We fought to stay alive."

I found my grandfather's brown overcoat in his attic, a heavy garment so long it draped behind me like a sad monarch's cape. It never occurred to me then what he might have felt as he lived inside this coat, inside a boxcar inside a land that not even a Great Lakes winter could have prepared him for, and the Great Lakes winter is not to be trifled with. I took, or was given, I don't remember which, a leather belt with a strap that went up and over the shoulder. For some reason, boys are always drawn to things that strap over the shoulder—guitars, rifles, backpacks—and by these things they are allowed to test the weight of whom they might someday become—musicians, soldiers, wanderers.

My grandfather never talked about it, or not to me anyway. He was an engineer first, a man of utility and order and who gave no truck to sadness or complaint. He was also a man of cold, frozen places, of the Great Lakes, which in winter offer something more pure even than the deepest meditation: infinite, white, terrible ice. These lakes aren't flat when they freeze. Their edges are frozen images of turmoil, waves and swells and garbage-flecked foam, clenched, caught unawares by the hard freeze. To gaze upon this is to set the mind first to flatness then to practicality then invention. Men from the Great Lakes region do not seek therapy, and not because doing so would bring them discomfort or shame, but because it is unnecessary. The winters here isolate everything but our troubles and allow the time and emptiness to solve them or find a place to hide them forever.

So my grandfather lived his life. When he needed a table saw to build his workshop, he worked out the puzzle in his head: build the saw first. He wrote a little booklet of his own—*Home Workshop Handbook*—and copied it and offered it "to anyone foolish enough to send name and address and one dollar to cover cost of prints." The pages are filled with uncanny practicality, handwritten in the precise block script common to engineers and draftsmen, detailing the properties of glues and adhesives; recommended drilling speeds for various materials; maximum spans for joists and rafters; lumber grades, nail sizes, wire gauges, and so on and so on.

The work is painstaking and tedious and raises the question why, which he answers in a brief, matter-of-fact introduction: "If this data had been readily available years ago, it might have prevented several poorly glued joints, burned drills, broken screws, and sloppy shellac jobs."

After my grandmother died and he had to start cooking for himself, he took a shine to prefab, frozen supermarket dinners. But they were too big for one serving, so he took them to the basement, fired up that homemade saw, and sliced the frozen slabs in half.

By the time my dad returned home, grinning and caked in white, we'd flung layer after layer of snow onto the continuous mound that wrapped the edge of the driveway, growing and growing. He came right into step with us and we continued to try to scrape away what the night had left behind. The wind had calmed some and the snowfall abated, but not enough to settle the nerves. Nothing was moving, anywhere. Not a single car had passed our house all day, and the sounds of digging and scraping were distant, disconnected. The idea that all of this could have happened so unexpectedly, so quickly, so violently, and so completely disturbed us all, even my dad, I think, though he seemed invigorated by the challenge to set it right. Men like him are at their best when something needs unexpectedly to be fixed.

We worked until the driveway was clear, ready for whatever might come next, then Ralph and I, and our sister and our younger brother, began to dig again. We hollowed out a cave in a Volkswagen-size snow mound, scooping and shaping deeper and deeper, until we four could sit upright inside. Then we carved out another, then began a tunnel between them and then another, until we had a network like the tubes in a gerbil cage. The light inside was strange, an optical paradox: muted and radiant, opaque and incandescent, and the sound had a similar quality, compressed and private and complete. Even the temperature was ambiguous. The packed snow warmed like insulation, until the cold crept into the bones and refused to leave.

Later, when night had fallen, I went back out and crawled inside and lay there in the dark, in the snow cave. It smelled like mute earth. I felt as if I could stay there forever, in the peaceful silence that only cold can produce. I closed my eyes and allowed myself to be carried off.

We took turns on the sleds, sometimes riding double, sometimes the four of us piled one on top of the other in defiance of physical laws, teetering, elbows digging into backs, gathering just enough momentum for the cartoon spill. We rode on a golf course near our home, down a glorious hillside hooded with oaks and maples, deep into a valley with steep sides and one slope gentle enough to climb back up for another plunge. We rode this way into the afternoon, into the late shade of a complicated winter sky. The northern Ohio sky is perpetually overcast in wintertime, but the acclimated natives could pass a blind-test between the early dusk and the sunless midafternoon, just as a Las Vegas lounge lizard inside a casino can sense the difference between 3:00 a.m. and 3:00 p.m. This was different, though. The sky had darkened in a way we'd never before seen, as if its humors were out of balance, blackening it with blood or bile.

Three days in, and the blizzard had only worsened. We were lucky; we had power and heat. Even so, we were isolated. Schools were closed, with no clue to when they might reopen. Most people couldn't go anywhere. Many were stranded wherever they had been when the storm hit. Those who did go out often had to turn back. It was hard to understand anymore whether this was an adventure.

Nature will always provide the best metaphors, and here amid the chaos, with the barometer lower than it had ever before been, was a strange coherence. Two weeks before this historic storm, Goodyear announced it was closing its main Akron factory. Nearly fourteen hundred people would be put out of work. A month later, Firestone would announce it was closing its big Akron plant, eliminating twelve hundred jobs. That year, 1978, four thousand people would lose their jobs in a city defined more than anything else by its work.

But as children, we didn't understand all that any more than we understood the barometer. What we understood was the velocity of steel and plastic on ass-groomed ice, caterwauling down the hills, cutting hard into turns and skidding, sideways stops, imagining ourselves at Innsbruck: Dorothy Hamill; Franz Klammer; Rosi Mittermaier. We'd brought along a pair of skis and tried those too, but the sleds were the thing, the flat-bottomed ones shooting us down the hills.

Our fingers and toes were deadened and impliable, such that the walk home was filled with complaining and the calculation of how bad these digits would burn when we filled the tub with hot water for the thaw. We played a game of frostbite one-upmanship, insisting nerve damage or blackened skin or amputation was imminent. As we pulled our sleds across the white fairways and greens, the sky began to take on an eerie darkness and suddenly more snow came, not floating, but crashing down, handfuls thrown by the lesser angels and saints, the simmering ones, disgruntled seraphim of the back-office operation whose task it was to remind us that ours is, every so often, a petulant God. And that's when I heard, for the first time in my experience of Ohio snowstorms, thunder.

We stumbled toward home in ragged formation, trudging faster through the snow. If you have never experienced an electrical blizzard, it is flat-out unnerving. The difference between thunder in a rainstorm and thunder in a snowstorm is the difference between Jimi Hendrix and Black Sabbath. It is bowling balls hurled toward hell.

We all started to run, pretending not to panic, until we made it home.

Days. Days. Somewhere out there the trucker melted more snow, drawing oxygen through that tube. A meteorologist was stuck at the airport, unable to get home—the weatherman himself stranded by the weather. He was taping extra pages onto his chart, the valley of the barometer so low it went to the bottom of the paper scroll and beyond. Somewhere, people were dying and had died.

Faith and belief are not the same thing, and anyone who has lain inside a snow cave at night in the dark of the American Midwest knows this. Faith is the promise of what might be. It is the blood brother of hope. Belief is pragmatism in isolation; it is what exists even if the world doesn't know you're there and never will. That's something more like the place I knew.

Our igloos lasted till Easter, the packed crust holding its form and the burrows inside abandoned. Eventually, their roofs collapsed or melted through. Rain got to them. Mud and black twigs pushed up from underneath. We kicked at them, resentful of the lost thrill. And then that day came, the day no one around here ever really believes will arrive, a day drunk, stumbling home from late winter, glasses cracked, salt-stained boots kicking the cans of hard times down the storm sewer. Sun and warmth, riding like a white-hatted parasite on the spiny back of a cold breeze, euthanizing the briny, primordial ice clenched to the curb until it bleeds its last.

For one day in Ohio, we get something whispering low in our ear, something hard to appreciate unless you've been through the Delta lows and Alberta clippers. The sun comes with an offer, one we are never sure we deserve. We have waited, we have waited, we have waited, and finally it comes and we have no choice but to accept this, our fate: the discomfort of grace.

THE LAKE EFFECT

Have you ever seen Lake Erie in the winter? It's the strangest thing. It freezes, as water will do in places this cold, but it doesn't freeze flat and calm, like Norwegian fjords or Frostian ponds. It freezes in gnarls of turmoil, as if someone said, "Hey, Great Lake, if you keep twisting your face like that it'll freeze that wa—"

And then it does.

The water gets all heavy and slushy but continues to churn, defiant, dauntless, pissed off, slower and slower, and then, just like that, it loses the fight, froth and waves and swells caught midmotion. I once stood on a wind-whipped Cleveland beach and saw a plastic diaper sticking up from the crust of ice at the edge and wished that the water had been able to churn one final time to save us both—the lake and me—from the unpleasantness. It was ugly as hell and it made me smile.

The winter of my sixteenth year, my dad got tickets to a football play-off game in Cleveland, the Browns against the Oakland Raiders. He and my two brothers and I rode up in one of his company's beat-up surveying vans, all of us bundled against the cold. My dad always bought vehicles with a profound antithesis of style: three-on-the-tree, pie-pan hubcapped, olive-drab tin boxes with a blank plate where the AM radio belonged. Hard vinyl bench seats. No carpet. No ceiling padding. Even with the heat on full blast, the inside of the van felt like a meat locker. The interior was caked with dried mud and smelled strongly of last summer's mosquito repellent, cut with the sweet lumbery pine of the wooden property stakes that clattered around in the rear. My older brother, Ralph, had tied his orange plastic, kid-size Browns helmet to the top of the van with clothesline. Slapped together on the cheap, we looked like everyone else driving into Cleveland that day.

There was never any color in the thirty miles of sky between Akron and Cleveland. It was a masterpiece of monochrome. Until you hit the city limits. There, the celestial flatness was spiked by a huge steel-factory smokestack with giant, fantastical flames roaring out its top. It looked exactly like hell and smelled worse. That's how we knew we were in Cleveland.

The temperature that day was four degrees; the windchill was thirty-six below. At the time, it was the second-coldest NFL play-off game ever played, which is uncannily correct. When you live in a place like this, you come to understand that we are never first. In anything. Not even misery. The second-most-frigid game in history? Yes. Exactly.

We parked as close as we could get to the stadium, which stood like some outpost of the Great Depression at the edge of Lake Erie's polluted, gunmetal waters. My dad had a spare pair of galoshes in the back of the truck, surveyor's boots. Before we locked up and started our walk to the stadium, he told me to put them on, but I refused. They didn't look cool. I was wearing my black, high-top Chuck Taylors, and there was no way I'd be seen in front of eighty thousand people sporting those hideous boots.

I'd never been to a Browns game before. I had no idea that the entire crowd would be dressed like some hybrid of a Dickens backstreet throng and a postapocalyptic hunting party. Here, camouflage was the mark of a Sunday dandy. These fans, three abreast on the sidewalk, shuffling toward Cleveland Municipal Stadium, were a cattle call of dull parkas topped with bulbous, oversize jerseys; fatsos in earflaps; drunks with double-layered blankets wrapped crooked around their torsos. Meaty men layered in flannel with two-week beards and stretched-out stocking caps. Women in mismatched gloves and padded hunting pants. They looked like a rogue regiment of Michelin Men. We joined them in the long, slow walk up East Ninth Street toward the colorless, hulking stadium, its countless tons of dumped concrete tracked with wooden seats.

I, still clinging to the potential street credibility of my footwear, was a decided outsider. I was casually interested in the Browns, in football, in sports. But as family dynamics go, I was a rank amateur. While I was reading Sherlock Holmes stories, my brother Ralph was memorizing the Browns media guide. His favorite pastime was being quizzed on arcane roster details:

Brian Sipe?
Quarterback! Number seventeen! San Diego State!
Major?
Architecture!
Dave Logan?
Receiver! Number eighty-five! University of Colorado!
Hometown?
Fargo! North Dakota!
And so on.

Not until we approached the stadium gates did I begin to feel something of the upsweep. And then there it was, as sudden and profound as the olfactory poignancy of a hog pen: the spirit of thousands, roughing out their ardor. The city smelled of barrel fires and roasted hot dogs and cold wool: the aluminum tang of a Cleveland January. But the sound is what defined the day, spontaneous group cheers delivered in bellowing choruses:

Here we go, Brownies, here we go! Whoo! Whoo!

We made our way through the gate and entered the immense, creaky, old concourse, pigeons roosting in the rafters above, paint cracked and peeling from the supports, piss trickling from the restroom troughs. The sound here intensified, like a freight train in a tunnel.

Let's go, Browns!
Let's go, Browns!
Let's go, Browns!

They cared, but even with something as overt as football, it wasn't entirely clear what they cared about. It seemed to be more than just the outcome of the game. We climbed the cement stairs to the bleachers, entering a vast, roaring stadium, ungodly cold. There was a rancid spice of hot chocolate and cigar smoke. From our seats behind the goalpost, I could see mounds of snow plowed along the sidelines, where the players, all with long sleeves under their jerseys, danced in place, blowing thick steam into their hands, waiting for the game to start. They seemed to move in slow motion. The playing surface looked different from how it did on television, and my dad explained to me that it was mostly dirt, but the groundskeepers painted it green to look better on camera.

Three men behind us were passing a thermos back and forth, and when the game began and the Raiders quarterback, Jim

Plunkett, took the field, one of them started hooting out, "Ya fuckin' Indian!"

The reference was loose at best. Plunkett's parents were Mexican American. But that mattered little. As the game went on, "fuckin' Indian" rolled from the trio of thermos drinkers behind us nearly as often as the deafening, hair-raising roar of *"DEE-FENSE"* overtook the stadium. If I was looking for a sound to define my day, that chant was the answer. It would begin small, somewhere indistinct, like a random match dropped in a dry forest, a single voice: *"Dee-fense."* A section of the stadium would call back in response, *"DEE-fense!"* Then half the stadium, and by the fourth or fifth round, the syllables would thunder—*"DEE! FENSE!"*—from deep in the guts of every one of the eighty thousand of us, a bellow of shared passion for stopping someone who was trying to push us around.

We could do it with our voices. We could stop the Raiders. We were vital. All we had to do was make ourselves known, to roar back into the mouth of Lake Erie.

The cold was brutal. I couldn't understand how the players were able to catch a hard football or run into one another. Everything I touched felt as if it would shatter. My eyeballs were made of candy glass. My lips were hardened Silly Putty. Packed tight between my brothers, I kept dropping to my seat to rub my hands together between my knees. By the end of the first quarter, I couldn't feel my toes and was nearly in tears as I bounced on the soles of my thin, woeful sneakers, desperate for warmth.

"I told you, you should have put on those boots," my dad said.

I refused to admit my pride.

Down on the field, the players seemed to be playing against the weather even more than themselves. Brian Sipe, the Browns quarterback, the SoCal native, looked desperate, with a turtleneck underneath his jersey, hands crammed into pockets sewn to the front. He looked as cold as I felt. When he dropped back to pass and tried to set his feet, he would slide on the icy brown-green surface. Offense was nearly nonexistent. Running plays looked like the ones my brother and I concocted on the vibrating metal sheet of our Coleco Electronic Football game, stiff-armed footballers pushing chaotically against one another without advancing. The two teams traded punts and interceptions, neither ever really moving the ball.

Halfway through the second quarter, I couldn't take the cold anymore and my dad sent me down to walk around in the concourse, where he thought it might be a little warmer. He didn't want me to go alone, but there was no way he was missing this. So my eleven-year-old brother, Louis, and I tramped down the stairs to the filthy promenade. It smelled like beer and piss and the flaccid perfume of boiled frankfurters. As we made our way through the interior, the sound of the slightly distant crowd was almost haunting:

"DEE-FENSE . . . DEE-FENSE . . . DEE-FENSE . . ."

But then, all at once, it changed. The sound rose above its already-impossible volume, a cacophonous roar. Something was happening . . . something big . . . something from which we had been omitted.

Louis looked at me.

"Shit," he said, a word he'd just learned from the thermos drinkers.

He knew I'd made him miss something, and even then his freckled baby face seemed to reveal a bitter wisdom, that this was something he would regret in something like a historic way. We raced back to our section, catching the scoreboard on the way.

Browns: 6

Raiders: 0

"You missed it!" Ralph screamed, wild-eyed, holding his hands against the sides of his stocking cap. "Bolton intercepted! He ran it back for a touchdown!"

The three men behind us were a tangle of arms and blankets and slaps and head bumps.

"Take that, ya fuckin' Indian!"

The Browns lined up to kick the extra point. As Don Cockroft gingerly made his approach on the frozen mud, a Raiders player blasted through the line and blocked the kick.

The game continued on this way, a constant struggle for footing, for position, for inches of advantage. Failure. Failure. Failure. All afternoon, the wind kept ripping in from Lake Erie. The old concrete of Municipal Stadium felt like glacial ice and it just hurt, all of it: the cold, the frustration, the brutal brotherhood of violence.

By the fourth quarter, the thermos drinkers had fallen into bouts of slurred, profane nonsense, blasting racist spittle toward Plunkett. The game had continued in a series of jabs and punts and miscues. Sipe threw an interception. Reggie Rucker dropped a touchdown pass in the end zone. Cockroft missed a field goal. Plunkett was sacked and fumbled. Cockroft missed another. The Raiders crashed clumsily into the end zone.

The Browns were down 14–12 with less than a minute to go. Finally finding a frantic groove, they had driven the ball to the Raiders' 13-yard line. It was third down. Sipe called a time-out. Everyone in the stadium was standing, bobbing with anticipation. Eighty thousand of us. Although I was squeezed parka-to-parka among the men of my family, I didn't feel warm, but I did feel something oddly similar to warmth: a shared coldness. Many of the seats in that ungainly stadium were "obstructed view," and part of the nuance of viewing a game there was adjusting position to see around the rusty, paint-chipped posts and I beams supporting the upper decks. We were all huddled close, the swish of nylon against nylon, the heavy murmur of anticipation, all of us sharing a calculation of the odds. All we needed was a field goal. No farther than an extra point. Then hold the Raiders for the remaining few seconds and this will all have been worth it.

The offense came back out onto the field. They lined up tight. Sipe raised his arms wide as he approached the line, trying to quiet the crowd. He leaned over the center, received the snap, looked across the end zone, drew back his arm, and released. The ball headed toward the goal line, toward the corner, toward tight end Ozzie Newsome, but it didn't look right, didn't zip through the air, was wobbling, caught up in the lake-effect wind, just long enough for a stumbling white jersey to cut in front of Newsome, the ball absorbed into the stickum-slathered arms of one of the Raiders, of someone who would be flying straight to California after this was done.

Intercepted.

The stadium fell silent. Browns players shrank from the celebration. The Raiders ran out the remaining seconds. It was over. Three weeks later they would win the Super Bowl. Everyone around us, wrapped in blankets and ponchos, looked dazed. What happened? We would soon learn that during the time-out, head coach Sam Rutigliano had called for a pass to the corner of the end zone, a play called Red Right 88. If no one was open, he'd told Sipe, "Throw it to the blonde in the second row." That would leave one more play for the chip-shot field goal. But Sipe had tried to force the throw, and that was that. He tried because he believed, and that was the biggest mistake. He should have known.

But that's what we do best. We believe. We come by this honestly. Because it's not failure that we know. It's something different, more complex, maybe worse: the feeling of almost winning.

In the years that followed it would become galvanized truth.

In 1987, the Browns played the Denver Broncos for the AFC Championship at old Municipal Stadium. With the clock ticking down and the Browns in the lead, John Elway led the Broncos on an impossible (not improbable; *impossible*) 98-yard drive, which became known as The Drive, to win the right to go to the Super Bowl. It's regarded as one of the worst defensive letdowns in pro football history.

In 1988, the two teams met again in the AFC Championship. As the Browns were about to score a last-minute, game-tying touchdown, running back Earnest Byner fumbled at the 3-yard line to lose the game, in a turn of events that became known as The Fumble. The Broncos took over the ball with a minute remaining and went to the Super Bowl. It's considered one of the most monumental collapses in pro football history.

In 1989, with the last second ticking off the clock and the best Cleveland Cavaliers team we'd ever known leading by 1 point and about to advance in the NBA play-offs, Michael Jordan rose above a double-team to hit a shot now known as The Shot to win the game. It is considered one of the greatest clutch plays in the history of all American sports. All we remember is the physical despair of Craig Ehlo, the Cavs' player over whose desperate up-stretched arms Jordan had just made history, Jordan leaping euphorically, Ehlo collapsing to the floor, hands clenching for something that wasn't there.

And so we have come to understand this bipolar choice we are offered: we could embrace impossible hope, or impossible hopelessness. But each of us had to choose. You can't stand in a frozen, zero-sum concrete ring and be in the middle.

Through all this, we have become known as a place that always loses.

But that's not how I see it.

I'm from a place that always almost wins.

ALL STARS

If you had to pick a single visual icon to represent the past century of Americana, I doubt you could do better than the Converse Chuck Taylor. The main trait of this seemingly uncomplicated canvas sneaker is not just how succinctly it represents the scope of American culture, but also how broadly. Iconic since its introduction in 1917, the shoe originally called the Converse All Star has offered street credibility to the entire range of American situations: a little boy in a Norman Rockwell painting; Larry Bird as the Hick from French Lick; a teenager in a mosh pit; a grunt on a Parris Island obstacle course; a Catholic schoolgirl; an aging rock star with a new album and an updated haircut; Whoopi Goldberg in an Oscar-night pantsuit; a new arrival at clown school. Like English ivy, the All Star arrived pure and then began to adapt.

For a long time, the shoes came only in two colors, white and black, like Hollywood cowboy hats. America became more colorful, and Converse followed, offering hues that eventually transcended color and would be better described as flavors: Cinnamon, Cantaloupe, Lilac, Amaranth, and Mud. Much like Jimi Hendrix, the All Star has dabbled in leather, hemp, and flames. It has reshaped itself to every new purpose without changing shape at all, tracing an inscrutable line from the ABA to CBGB. As much as anything in our culture, the Converse All Star is *itself*. And this is both despite and because it is entirely unsuitable for its original purpose.

The Chuck Taylor was one of the first shoes specifically

designed for basketball. In nearly a century since, it has proven itself apt to everything *except* basketball. This is a shoe with the arch support of an emery board, the shock absorption of a Post-it note, and the breathability of a wet suit. That it endures despite itself suggests it has something to prove, something to overcome, which might be its most American quality.

There is one thing, however, that's even more American than the Chuck Taylor: the art of marketing. And there may be no better fable of that art than the fable of Chuck Taylor himself.

Chuck Taylor (it seems unthinkable to refer to him by anything other than his full name) is the second-most-famous basketball player ever to come from Akron, Ohio. Most people don't know he even played basketball. That's understandable. He didn't play much. A lot of people probably assume he's not even a real person, but rather a marketing phantom, like Mrs. Butterworth or Chef Boyardee.

That's understandable too, because his identity is confined to that signature inside the circle of the All Star logo. *Chuck Taylor* is an enigma akin to the 33 on the back of a Rolling Rock bottle and the arm and hammer on the baking-soda box. This may be the only athletic shoe in existence whose celebrity namesake is someone nobody knows anything about—or even whether it's a real person at all. (Rod Laver is the exception that proves this point.) Air Jordans and Shaqs exist only because the athletes are famous. Conversely (so to speak), the real man named Chuck Taylor only exists in American memory because his shoes are famous.

In that sense then, he is both: a real person, and a marketing phantom.

Here is a peculiar identity trait: the fear that you have no identity at all. Places in the American Midwest seem to carry this as a genetic presumption. In fact, most places referred to as Midwestern shy away from the term, afraid such a broad, amorphous definition will counteract its purpose, leading to a misinterpretation, a stereotype, or an insult. We are so used to being misunderstood that we react preemptively. Our personalities are delicate and complex. My city is particularly stricken—a place known for most of the twentieth century as the Rubber Capital of the World was stunningly, completely stripped of that identity by virtue of a swift and profound industrial collapse. We were something, we were Known, like Firestone, and then, in a few years, we found ourselves with no idea of who we were or what was to become of us. As a result, we have tended toward a pathological compulsion to seize homegrown cultural coattails. To associate ourselves with something that would help us to explain ourselves to the wider world. To call out collectively like the Whos down in Whoville, "We are here! We are here!"

Therefore, part of the local neurosis is a habit of identifying celebrities (no matter how minor) with ties (no matter how tenuous) to Akron, and at every opportunity making mention of this. Hugh Downs lived in Akron briefly as an infant, yet we claim him as a native son. Here's a conversation I've heard too many times to dismiss.

"Oh, I see Hugh Downs is coming back for another season on *20/20*."

"He's from Akron, you know. . . ."

I've observed this in other places too, the way people from Buffalo will perk up when someone mentions Frank Lloyd Wright and impulsively interject, "He's from Buffalo."

Liberace is from Milwaukee. Mario Andretti is from Allentown. Bob Eubanks is from Flint. You have no idea how important this is.

Pittsburgh, Lord. Andy Warhol famously *hated* the place, his hometown. But Andy Warhol became famous and Pittsburgh dutifully named a bridge after him and built his museum.

Is Akron the birthplace of the Chuck Taylor? Hell yes. Let me tell you how.

Chuck Taylor is not from Akron, but his basketball career would be irrelevant were it not for Akron, and his basketball career (a surprisingly brief one) was what led to everything else. Taylor played one season—1920–21—for a team called the Akron Firestone Non-Skids, a thick-thighed young man in striped socks and a tight tank top emblazoned with a stylized *F.* This was an industrial-league professional basketball team that, not surprisingly, was named after an automobile tire. The Firestone product from which the team took its name was itself a stroke of marketing genius. In the early era of the tire industry, competition among the American manufacturers, all based in Akron, was fierce. So in 1908, company founder Harvey S. Firestone, in a meeting with his design engineers, came up with the idea for a new tread pattern, one that would use raised lettering as the actual tread. As the story goes, he reached for a scrap of paper on his desk and, writing in a diagonal descent, showed them the pattern:

FIRESTONE
    NON
        SKID

An elegant solution: the words described their function, the function derived from the words.

From this signature product came the name of the company basketball team. The Non-Skids thrived in the years between the two World Wars. In 1939, the team (along with its Goodyear counterpart, the Wingfoots) became a charter member of the National Basketball League, which a dozen years later would merge into the NBA.

It appears from his statistics and the historical record that Chuck Taylor was not a significantly impactful basketball player. He made one key shot to win one important game and was celebrated for that moment, but otherwise the accolades are thin. Some sources even question whether he played as much pro basketball as his record asserts. Certainly it's doubtful that he was ever a "famous" basketball player. Such a thing didn't exist in 1921, at least not as we now understand it.

In the 2006 biography *Chuck Taylor, All Star: The True Story of the Man behind the Most Famous Athletic Shoe in History*, author Abraham Aamidor describes the Akron year as "a watershed in Chuck Taylor's playing days."

Aamidor writes, "What Chuck had learned in Akron, besides some pointers from [coach Paul] Sheeks and skills gained in competitive play, was the art of self promotion."

It was a watershed in a different way as well. Taylor was off the team and out of town after a single season. The reason is not known; Aamidor speculates he may have been cut.

So Chuck Taylor, with dubious athletic accomplishments, left Akron with a handful of clippings from the local newspaper and a photograph of himself posing with the Non-Skids, documents he produced upon arriving at his next stop—Detroit—where he portrayed himself as a sports celebrity. Detroit was a bigger playing field with its own share of company teams, and Taylor soon picked up with a team called the Rayls, named after the sporting-goods store that was its sponsor. The connection to a retailer that likely carried athletic shoes is presumably what led to the ambitious young man's next move, the following year, to Chicago, where he was hired by Converse. He soon hit the road, selling All Star sneakers through a series of basketball clinics he ran—his purported expertise based on his record as a professional basketball player. With a résumé that bordered on a bait and switch, he thrived.

In 1932, as a show of appreciation for his sales acumen, Converse put Chuck Taylor's neat cursive signature on the All Star logo. His may be the most convoluted endorsement deal in the history of sports merchandise: the shoe named for the star salesman, who became a salesman because of his perceived basketball stardom, which was created out of a sense of salesmanship. A circle of paradoxes. The more that is understood about his name on the round patch, then, the more enigmatic it becomes.

It's worth mentioning that at about the same time Chuck Taylor was beginning his career with Converse, Jack Purcell, a champion badminton player, designed a similar canvas sneaker for Firestone's crosstown rival B. F. Goodrich, which had a shoe division. (For the record, yes, in the 1930s, the idea of a "famous" badminton player was even less conceivable than that of a "famous" basketball player.) The Jack Purcell sneaker played out the next thirty-five years as a sort of second cousin to the Chuck Taylor. Eventually, in 1970, Converse bought that brand as well, merging an odd couple of legends.

My favorite image of Converse All Stars as basketball shoes is from the 1961 Disney movie *The Absent-Minded Professor*, a film in which the fictional Medfield College basketball team applied the semi-magical polymer compound "flubber" to the bottom of their Chuck Taylors, allowing them to prodigiously sky. Flubber, which doesn't actually exist, is a discovery by Medfield professor Ned Brainard (Fred MacMurray), who accidentally adds energy, rather than subtracts it, while writing out the formula for enthalpy. The resulting compound bounces like rubber, gaining energy with each successive bounce.

What I love about this story is my absolute certainty that if flubber did exist, it would have been invented in Akron. I once asked one of the world's leading experts on flubber-related chemistry if flubber could exist. Dr. Frank Kelley, who at the time was the dean of the college of polymer science and engineering at the University of Akron and is also literally a rocket scientist, not only entertained the notion, but did some calculating on my behalf.

Eventually, he concluded that, no, the physical law of the conservation of energy would not allow such a substance. Energy can't be created. But the scientific answer was not a disappointment. That Dr. Kelley understood the question, understood the worth of grasping toward the fantastic, even the impossible, of entertaining the most distant possibility of connection—that was the true answer.

KAREEM'S THE ONE
WITH THE GLASSES, RIGHT?

There really was no other way to deal with the situation than to look the tall, naked black man directly in the eye. He wanted a hot dog. I couldn't just ignore him.

In a situation like that, the best option is to go with direct, locked-on, no-way-is-my-gaze-wandering-here-sir eye contact. Even so, for a preternaturally shy seventeen-year-old who still had trouble with any public encounter that involved anything other than pretending to be somewhere else, this was going to be a challenge.

Add to this that I'd had little actual contact with any black people in my mostly sheltered lifetime, nor with naked people in general, my discomfort was as urgent as it was complex.

"Mustard?" I asked.

He reached into the long fur coat hanging in his wooden stall and pulled out a handful of bills. I tried not to glance down at the money, keeping my eyes focused on his, even though his hardly seemed aware that I existed.

He may well have been famous. I didn't know. Among my many professional liabilities was that I was, and probably remain, the only employee in the history of the National Basketball Association who didn't know anything about basketball, nor about basketball players nor the sport's emergent cultural importance nor any of the basic rules or techniques of the game. I was a Cleveland Cavaliers ball boy who possessed no intrinsic loyalty to the home team and who, most nights, was more interested in the contents of the Gatorade bucket than the presence of Larry Bird or Kareem Abdul-Jabbar in the visitors' locker room. I identified Abdul-Jabbar as "the guy with the goggles" and Bird as "the guy who really should reconsider that mustache." I did have a certain fascination for Cornbread Maxwell, but only because he had a cool name and seemed like a nice person. But then, the same could be said of my English teacher, Sister Noel. It had nothing to do with his talent or fame. Those things were lost on me.

Some guys would give you exactly what it cost to go buy them a hot dog, and some would give you a random handful of crumpled bills and tell you to keep the change. This was usually how I reckoned which ones were famous and which ones were not. In this case, I wasn't aware of how much I had been handed because to have looked down at the cash would have been to risk seeing more than my teenage, inadequate self could bear, so I quickly closed my fingers over the money and turned to leave.

"Hey, kid—how much did I give you?"

I looked into my hand and answered sideways toward the floor, "Five."

"Get me two."

Under any circumstances, I suppose, being a ball boy for an NBA team is an unusual first job. I wasn't aware of that then, inasmuch as no teenager is aware of the unusualness of his life until other people start to point it out to him, a bittersweet gift that, so far, had not been granted to me. It was a job. I was paid $15 and two complimentary tickets per game. Because the tickets often went unused, I didn't consider them part of my compensation package. I did, however, value the half-used rolls of athletic tape I often scrounged from the trainer's-room floor. With better adhesion than masking tape, it was useful for hanging posters on my bedroom wall. Even on the most humid summer days, James Dean and the Police stayed put.

The main focus of my work was to touch nothing.

This seemed the only prudent approach to a working life in a room full of physically superior men who were naked about 40 percent of the time, whose own sense of their bodies was at once primitive and evolved, the floor around them littered with the ubiquity of their constantly changing shells, from street clothes to ankle wraps to uniforms to sweats to naked for showers to towels to ice packs to street clothes again: sweat-soaked socks and sodden jockstraps, unraveled bandages and spent towels, satiny uniforms stewing in the funk of blood, snot, pasty perspiration, and midshelf cologne.

Another kid seemed positively charged by this atmosphere, walking through the locker room gathering great handfuls of "socks and jocks," a term he used as though he were the maître d' and it were the house specialty. He had a habit of tapping players' bottoms with all the cheerful encouragement of a father teaching his son to ride a bike and calling them either by their known nicknames or the impromptu handles that came to him on the wings of some locker room Muse: *Bingo! A.C.! Footsie! Sweets!*

I had learned to keep my fingernails on the long side so that when I did have to pick up anything dropped on the floor, I could use them as a set of tweezers, keeping to a minimum the contact between my own skin and another man's intimate apparel.

Look—I'll just come right out and say it: I once witnessed a seven-foot center trying to pop the pimples on his back, a physically difficult task even for a gifted professional athlete. My perspective on the entire matter of my employment was cast.

*   *   *

I knew I was surrounded by absurdity, but I may have been the only member of the organization with absolutely no context for how profound the situation actually was. I wasn't aware that I had happened into one of the most deranged and downtrodden locker rooms in the history of the NBA, that of the early-1980s Cleveland Cavaliers. I wasn't aware that the team was on its way toward what was then the longest losing streak in NBA history: twenty-four games. I wasn't aware that it was unusual for only two thousand fans to show up for a pro basketball game in a twenty-thousand-seat arena. Nor did I recognize that my boss— Ted Stepien, a fleshy millionaire with a long, sparse comb-over, oversize, squarish glasses, and a nasal whine that sounded like milk curdling—was considered by many to be the worst owner of any franchise in the history of American professional athletics. (He gained sports immortality by virtue of the NBA's "Stepien Rule," which limits an owner's ability to trade future first-round draft picks. By the time the emergency legislation was instituted by league officials, Stepien had given away nearly a decade's worth of first-rounders, offering them like shore-leave cash for whatever journeymen were available. His approach to catching lightning in a bottle, it seemed, was to fling the bottles wildly off a cliff.)

I knew my situation was odd, but it had nothing to do with any of that. I knew my situation was odd because I was aware enough to know something was going on that I couldn't understand, but not aware enough to know what it was. (This, incidentally, is a good description of what it feels like to be seventeen years old.) Even among all these notable misfits, I was an outsider. Where others were baffled by the then-lavish $700,000 salaries the owner was paying to the likes of James Edwards and Scott

Wedman, I was confounded by this "three seconds" Mr. Stepien was constantly carping about from his floor seat behind the basket. For all the problems of his franchise, this rule restricting how long an offensive player could stand in the free-throw lane seemed to be the singular thing Stepien cared about. Or maybe even knew about.

"Three seconds! Hey! Three seconds on that guy! C'*mon*! Threeee secondsssss!"

Stepien—who not only sat in on half-time meetings, but also sometimes tried to diagram plays, to the bewilderment of almost everyone else—went through four coaches in a single season. One of them, Chuck Daly, celebrated his firing with champagne. Stepien predicted Daly would never again have such an opportunity as he'd been offered in Cleveland; Daly almost immediately established a dynasty as coach of the Detroit Pistons and is now in the Basketball Hall of Fame.

To me, that hyperactive rate of turnover was the definition of normal. I saw players and team employees come and go with the frequency of courthouse pigeons. By the time the third coach arrived, I just took it as a given that his days were numbered. I was far more intrigued by the way brand-new sneakers piled up in the dressing-room trash cans after games. Players undressed and just threw their sneakers into the garbage. Perfectly good leather Converse and Reeboks and Nikes. If only I wore a size 13.

Even to my perspective—which was something like that of a French Revolution time-traveler who found himself suddenly in an episode of *Miami Vice*—a clear, profoundly paradoxical moral conflict existed between frugality and wastefulness in the locker room. While the wastebaskets filled up with $100 sneakers, the refrigerator with the postgame food for the players was stocked with soggy, low-rent sandwiches—chip-chop and ham salad and the like, hand-wrapped in cellophane. Even as the owner threw lucrative contracts to the likes of an aging Bobby Wilkerson, the equipment guy had to reuse the name banners sewn to the backs of the uniforms. When Dave Robisch was unloaded from the team, the trainer's assistant carefully unstitched the panel and, on its blank reverse side, ironed the synthetic letters of the new guy's surname: C-A-L-V-I-N.

This tension grew as it became more and more clear that the team was in deep financial trouble. There were rumors that the astronomical payroll wasn't being met. We ball boys hadn't been paid in weeks, and because I had recently been named "head ball boy" (a promotion that was, at best, titular), the others were pressuring me to speak up on their behalf, which made me uncomfortable for many reasons.

"He fired Joe Tait."

"What?!"

"He did. He fired Tait."

"No way."

"Yeah way."

Even I knew this was huge. Joe Tait was the radio announcer for the Cavs, the only one they'd ever had, and to say he was the voice of the team is only a flimsy metaphoric cliché. He kind of *was* the team. My much more sports-oriented brother had an album of season audio highlights issued after the "Miracle in Richfield" year—1976. In our sports universe, this is what constituted a "miracle": the Cavaliers made the play-offs. They lost in the conference finals, but that didn't stop the legend, especially with Tait's modulated Midwestern twang providing the narration.

Tait was the perfect voice for a hard-bitten sports town, a decidedly unfancy man in a decidedly unfancy place. Devoid of modifiers and metaphors and unwilling to spin tall men into legends, he served his descriptions straight. He had only two catch-phrases: "Wham with the right hand!" and "Have a good night, everybody." One is meat, the other potatoes.

Most of that album is a collage of Tait's calling the action in a voice that sounds like an uncanny chamber quartet: bugle, trombone, bassoon, and kettle drum. And the whole thing comes to a climax in one of the greatest play-by-play ejaculations I've ever heard. Anyone who has lived in northeast Ohio for the past generation knows the call:

> *Bingo on the run . . . the gun . . . he shoots . . . no good . . .*
> *rebound Clemons! . . . Scooooorrrre!!!*

Because of the distorted euphoria of that final syllable, some circles of local conspiracy theorists still believe Tait is not actually bellowing "Score" but is screaming "Fuuuuuccccckkk!!!" in uncontrolled celebration, a theory that seems to be more a projection of desire—we want those who deliver our news to share our response to it—than plausible possibility.

We all knew Tait from the pressroom, a great big man in a sweater, unassuming, but also, by nature, commanding. He would acknowledge us, which was a particular demarcation. There were those who recognized you were there, and those who did not. Tait recognized us. So when word spread through the ball-boy ranks that the man commonly referred to as "the Voice of God" had been canned by Mr. Stepien, it was like hearing the president had been shot. The story we heard was that Tait had said something during one of the game broadcasts critical of Stepien—something that was almost impossible to avoid even in an objective account of the events of any given day.

Stepien responded to the public outcry by telling reporters that announcers are "a dime a dozen."

Joe Tait was reinstated after Stepien, having lost $15 million in three seasons, sold the team in 1983. Tait remained the voice of the Cavaliers until 2011 and is in the Broadcasters Hall of Fame.

Only one person seemed to openly recognize the absurdity of our collective situation. That was Don Ford, a benchwarmer who averaged 1.1 points and 9.6 minutes a game in the 1981–82 season. Ford had arrived from the Los Angeles Lakers in a player-and-picks deal that included, naturally, a swap of first-rounders. The Lakers received the Cavs' 1982 first-round pick, which they used to draft James Worthy, who almost immediately became a superstar and is now in the Basketball Hall of Fame. The Cavs received the Lakers' 1980 first-round pick, which they used to draft Chad Kinch, who played in forty-one games of professional basketball and was out of the NBA after one season.

Don Ford was pretty much the opposite of everyone I'd ever known: a handsome, lanky surfer-type from Santa Barbara with longish blond hair and a wry self-awareness. While his teammates spent their pregame hours getting treatment for sore joints and injuries, or reviewing stats, or clumsily insulting one another, Ford just sort of elaborately hung out. People whose entire lives have been defined by what they do with their bodies—athletes, cowboys, strippers, etc.—tend to have specific physical personalities. The basketball players I saw each exuded this dynamic. The big men expressed their bigness in every gesture, in the way, for instance, they pulled the snaps loose on their warm-up pants as though they were Vikings shaking out the broad sails. The point guards had a nimble precision even in the way they ate their postgame chip-chop sandwiches. Don Ford, however, was the only player I knew whose physical personality was one of expert relaxation. Even when he was on the court, he was loose and windblown.

One of my duties was to bring basketballs around the dressing room to be signed by all the team members. Everyone had his own curlicued scrawl, perfected over the years into nonchalance. Ford did too, but always added a little hipster dash, sometimes signing *Disco Don Ford* or *Devo Don Ford*. He was the only player who ever addressed me with what seemed like genuine interest. I didn't resent the others for their demeanors, which resided generally in the regions of distraction, disinterest, and dismay. Although I never came to understand the game they played for a living, I did come to understand the effect of their existence within it—something people rarely get to see, even in our era of deeply intense celebrity fascination. I came to understand the way public people create, by necessity, a force field of self-preservation. I saw what it was like for them not even to be able to step from the shower into a towel without someone coming up to ask for something—an interview, an autograph, a basketball to be signed. It's a skewed survival technique: to have to shield yourself from adoration. Realness, for them, had to be achieved through an artificial process.

Don Ford seemed unique because he seemed entirely real, aware not only of his own place in the world, but the places of those around him. (As an addendum, I never blamed pro athletes for being slightly out of touch with reality. The reality in the locker rooms I experienced was something like a bacteria to be avoided.) Ford would ask me questions, just small talk about school or my family or even, half-jokingly, what I thought of the team's chances that night. I would stiffen up and hate myself for not being able to just answer his questions, to be like him—cool and casual; knowing.

He seemed aware that we were all losers by association, and that it wasn't the worst thing in the world. In an interview one time, he referred to his team as the "Cleveland Cadavers." The local media picked up on it and a new nickname took hold: the Cadavaliers.

One night, Ford sat looking at his game check, leaning way back in the chair in front of his wooden locker stall. He wouldn't be with the team much longer—everyone knew that—but he had another year guaranteed on his contract.

"Mr. Stepien's gonna pay me to sit on the beach for a year," he said in a way that could only be described as cavalier.

I knew what a cavalier was. I'd devoted a great deal of my youth to reading about people who carried swords and wore capes and feathers and rode horses. As a result, I had yet another question about this enigmatic organization that employed me. My emergent sense of place told me I lived in a region fiercely proud of its grittiness and its blue-collar sensibilities and its disdain for foppishness and pretense. Even though the Cavaliers didn't actually play in Cleveland—they played in a cold, rigid concrete tank called the Coliseum (another curious non sequitur) in a rural suburb called Richfield—they were Cleveland's team, and the way I always knew we'd arrived in Cleveland on the highway from Akron was when I saw that tall, black, flaming steel-factory smokestack. None of this evoked the gallantry of the cavaliers I knew from books.

Other teams in the region had names like Browns (because the first coach was a hard-nosed genius named Brown and because brown is the color of mud and dried blood and also the sky above a factory) and Steelers (because steel is made here and beer cans and Camaro rims are made of steel) and Indians (because we have a wooden ear in matters of cultural sensitivity). Why Cleveland's basketball team would be called the Cavaliers remains almost as much a mystery to me as the three-second rule.

Ted Stepien did not name the team. That was done a decade before, when Cleveland entered the league. To his credit, he did have a knack not only for marketing—he'd made his fortune as founder of Nationwide Advertising Service—but specifically for marketing to the sorts of fans who comprised the northeast-Ohio sports-consumption market.

He adopted a polka for the team's fight song. At one end of the floor, dressed in tube tops, short-shorts, and pantyhose, he installed the Teddy Bears, vampish cheerleaders who were the owner's namesake, which gave the whole arrangement a daddy/daughter creepiness. Over on one side of the court was Superfan, a sort of everyman-slob-cheerleader whose gut bounced inside a too-tight, black T-shirt and whose gimmick was tearing apart beer cans with his teeth.

"Three seconds! Three seconds on that guy! Hey—three seconds, come on! Gene? Gene? Did you see that? Three seconds!"

Stepien's lament, coming from a floor seat behind the basket, would have cut through even a boisterous crowd, but often there were only a few thousand fans—the masochists and optimists that represent the demographic cornerstones of the Rust Belt—and the owner's incessant refrain was all the more prominent.

The play tumbled off to the other end of the court and I was left there with my towels and paper cups and my deluxe dust mop, folding tossed-aside warm-up pants and wondering why it was such an issue with him. I wasn't completely in the dark. I'd long before calculated that three seconds was three thousand milliseconds and one-twentieth of a minute and therefore one nine-hundred-sixtieth of a game, which is to say that I worked a lot of recreational math to pass the time as I sat blankly staring at the hardwood during another interminable third quarter. It was always the third quarter, always that time that is no time when you're working a job that holds nothing for you.

I could even see that dead time on the bench sometimes. I don't think anyone ever gave up, but when you're losing and you know too well what it feels like to lose, and you've been psychically prepared your entire life to win, you just want that loss to end. The seated players would sometimes gaze emptily as the drudgery continued up and down the court, as though trying to see back into their boyhood selves who dreamed of one day being here, doing this, and the wonder of it all.

I knew that the phrase *three seconds* represented some kind of violation because occasionally a whistle would blow and the whine from the floor seat would turn jubilant: "See? See? Three seconds! It's about time. . . ."

But what I never came to understand, and to this day still do not understand, is how, with the dizzying number of possible fouls—a hack over here, a push over there, a charge and a goaltend and an over-and-back—the referees could also possibly be running an internal clock measuring how long someone was positioned in the paint. The game moved so fast, I never saw anyone do *anything* for three seconds. Twenty hands and twenty feet and twenty elbows are on the floor at all times, each in constant motion, plus lines and arcs and planes to account for, such that it would take the mind of Euclid, the emotional resolve of Sgt. Rock, and the physical stamina of Bruce Jenner to keep it all together. Sometimes whole minutes would go by before I realized there'd been a substitution and I hadn't offered the returning player a towel and the requisite drink menu—"Water or Gatorade?"—to the back of a man who never turned to answer, just reached for what he needed.

*   *   *

We had not been paid in more than a month and some of the ball boys were pestering the trainer, who oversaw us, to do something. But what could he do? Rumors were spreading through the locker room and the cavernous back hallways of the Coliseum that *no one* was getting paid. Even if that wasn't true, we all understood that this was not an organization with any discernible justice system—or any discernible system at all. Things just sort of happened. Or didn't. All I knew was that whatever money was on the table was not worth the growing pressure from my colleagues to exert my "head ball boy" authority. Even if I was to make a stand, I didn't have a clue where to make it, nor to whom, nor how stands were made at all. I'd never been righteous a day in my life.

One of the other ball boys latched onto me as we went through our pregame duties—hauling buckets of ice to the locker room, helping the trainer set up his cart, distributing towels, folding warm-up suits, avoiding staph infection, etc.

"Stepien always hangs around courtside at halftime. Let's ask him."

"Ask him what?"

"For our checks."

"We can't do that."

"Sure we can. It's our money. It's only right."

I wanted to believe that this was true, that being right justified doing something that seemed entirely wrong. But I didn't believe that. The problem was that I wasn't clear about what I believed, about anything, and this is how I found myself at halftime, when I should have been dust-mopping my end of the court, instead approaching Ted Stepien, who stood talking to another man in a suit.

"Um. Mr. Stepien?"

He turned those big, square glasses in my direction.

"Uh, I was just wondering if, um, you could tell us when the ball boys were going to get paid . . . ?"

When I arrived for work the next night, the trainer called me into the back room.

"What were you thinking?"

I couldn't answer, partly because of the lump rising in my throat, but mostly because the question was its own answer. What was I thinking? I think. I wasn't. Thinking.

I knew what was coming next. I'd been fired. Stepien had just finished screaming at the trainer about how he'd been embarrassed by some ball boy whom he didn't ever want to see in the building again. I didn't argue. I left, making my way back through the locker room. A few players were already there, easing into another miserable night, big, long, misshapen men half in street clothes and half out, stretching overtaxed knees and pulling cricks from their necks, preparing themselves to be beaten once more.

I exited through the back door toward the parking lot. There, in the first row, was Mr. Stepien's big, shiny car. I slowed. I looked behind me. Then I walked toward the car, at first not sure what I was about to do, then with an idea, and then something like conviction.

I picked up my stride, and when I got to the car, I reached out for the driver's door handle, gave it a yank, and kept on walking, the car alarm blaring its nonsense with undue urgency.

Three seconds! Three seconds! Three seconds!

PART TWO

BE
APPROXIMATELY
YOURSELF

WE ALMOST WON.
WE ALMOST ALWAYS
ALMOST WIN.

-JOSH CRIBBS, CLEVELAND BROWNS

LOOKING FOR A NAME

More than anything else that summer, I needed a bowling shirt. This seemed like the most necessary thing in the world, or at least in Ohio. A bowling shirt with fanciful embroidery and a cryptic team sponsor's name stitched across the back, maybe a plumber or a garage, something involving the word *scooter*. A shirt with side vents and a contrasting yoke, made of good old-school rayon, with depth and heft. The weight of a cape, a habit, a mantle. Something the Stray Cats might wear to the diner for strong coffee in thick, white cups and cheeseburgers and unstudied flirtation. Something John Lurie would pluck at random from the bedside in a Jim Jarmusch joint. Something with *Perma-Prest* and *drip-dry* in the laundering instructions. Something with the right color scheme—black and red; turquoise and yellow; pink and almost anything. Maybe (dreaming here) *something with buttons shaped like dice*. And most important of all, a name above the pocket— Howie or Slim or Mack. The offer of personality.

At eighteen, in a factory town where bowling was as culturally significant as church, I recognized something authentic about such a shirt, something tangible and true, and also something circularly ironic, that it was the costume of some other culture than my own that was in fact the culture of which I was made, and to which I now aspired with what I imagined was irony. But, at eighteen, I didn't have much of a grasp on authenticity or irony or culture. Most of my spare time was spent looking for clues. And piles of discarded clothing were as good a place as any to start.

All of our information about what was cool came in fragments and obliquely. In the 1980s, the mass culture of three-network television and *Life* magazine was actively fracturing, but for the time being, subcultures traveled on foot. A great gap lay between the underground and the mainstream. This was the technological interlude before the Internet. In fact, this suspended moment at the end of a generalized, shared American culture was probably the thing that made the Internet *necessary*. As the top-down approach was disintegrating, the bottom-up was being conceived. In that in-between moment, however, Akron was the hinterlands. We knew this information existed, but found it agonizingly elusive. We were restless therefore in our yearning, knowing that tantalizing new ideas were creeping in beneath our feet. We wanted to know.

A newsstand at the mall carried *New York Rocker*, a low pulp fanzine I waited for monthly and devoured cover to cover, attempting to digest its secrets. *How to cuff my jeans. The Gun Club. Am I a sunglasses person? Human Switchboard. Talking Heads. The meaning of anger. Bow Wow Wow. Sturm und Drang. Lust.* But almost as soon as I'd made this a monthly pilgrimage, the magazine stopped appearing—gone, disappeared, a phantom. I stayed up late every night watching *Don Kirshner's Rock Concert* and the outlaw Pee-wee Herman on HBO and *Second City Television (SCTV)* reruns and, on the weekends, *New Wave Theatre* on the USA Network. These things emerged like little Brigadoons. As soon as I discovered *Rock Concert*, it was canceled. Pee-wee Herman's appearances were sporadic, hard to catch, and next thing I knew he surfaced reworked as a Saturday-morning network star. Every *SCTV* sighting seemed like a gift, a visit from Sasquatch. I happened, by total chance, upon MTV the night it debuted, and I really believed I'd discovered some obscure delight that no one else knew about or would ever know about. Akron was one of the first cities in the country to be wired for cable. We had it years before Manhattan, and while I'd like to think that made us pioneers, I think it was a greater indication that the channelers of culture recognized we needed it as a lifeline, that this information would be more precious to people like us, forsaken at the edge of Lake Erie, in the midst of the industrial wasteland.

So I had visual information that informed me *something* about a bowling shirt would be beneficial to my image (or lack thereof), and while I might not have known precisely what that meant, I did know where to look.

My friend Dave and I had been paying regular visits to the big, sprawling Goodwill store at the edge of the University of Akron campus. Our main purpose was to outfit ourselves for the Bank, a cavernous rock club in the middle of downtown that occupied the marble lobby and mahogany balcony of an abandoned bank. (Sometimes irony is unnecessary.) We were teenagers in a city that was fast losing its identity, ourselves just beginning to seek identities of our own. We needed outfits.

Dave was looking for a suit coat with skinny lapels and sleeves he could roll up in the manner of an English synth-pop bassist. And I had determined I would express my individuality via a secondhand shirt with another man's name trimmed over the heart.

Every time there is a monumental cultural shift, its spew lands in the Goodwill.

You don't have to look hard to find it, but you have to dig in deep to understand it; you have to enter the groove, slide your flattened hands between the fabric, layers upon layers, leafing through them like the living text of a place. But it's there: a story full of endings.

Slowly, it emerges from the chaos of high-school-band sweat-shirts and hospital-sponsored 5K freebie T-shirts and Myrtle Beach souvenirs: patterns and the meaningful breaking of pattern. So first I came to understand what belonged and then to understand what didn't belong. I came to understand that the racks and shelves contained more than just the usual hand-me-downs and castoffs. This Goodwill was Akron's central warehouse, so it received much of the unloaded ballast of our diaspora.

Akron had lost close to eight thousand factory jobs in the preceding decade, and forty thousand residents (which translates to roughly ten thousand bowlers). A lot of people were giving up. There was despair, but even more, there was an uneasy void. These people just vanished. Vaporized. All the layoffs and factory closings and civic collapses of the preceding decade had led to families' picking up and leaving, often headed South, where corporations were reestablishing manufacturing in nonunion settings, the right-to-work states. Often these departures happened abruptly, and often bitterly, and often in the kind of separation that doesn't want the burden of memory.

So among the knickknack floor lamps and Reader's Digest Condensed Books and discarded wooden crutches, we found too-recent high school yearbooks and frames with family pictures still inside and plastic, gold bowling trophies that ought to have been gathering dust in the attic of a house where someone ought to have stayed until retirement and then death. I found tools and album collections and golf clubs that I knew would only be left by a man who had to make a quick exit. I'd spent enough time in my grandfather's and father's exquisitely cluttered workshops to understand that men do not give their tools to Goodwill. It simply isn't done.

One of my most profound revelations came when I discovered three albums stacked together in a single Goodwill record bin: Elvis

Costello and the Attractions' *Armed Forces*, Adrian Belew's *Twang Bar King*, and Pete Townshend's *All the Best Cowboys Have Chinese Eyes*. There could be no accident about this. Those records, released within four years of one another, had to have come from the same collection. They had to have been in the collection of someone with specific, particular, rarefied taste, someone who really cared. They were not records that would have been discarded so soon after their release and their astute purchase. They were not records that belonged in a Goodwill. Not unless something had prompted a sudden liquidation. I would have bought them anyway, because, at 25¢ apiece, they represented a true windfall. But even more I bought them to honor whatever regrets had led to their present situation, and to keep them the way they belonged. When I took them home, I put them in the wooden crate with my other albums, making certain to stack them together, intact.

Akron, and places like Akron, are unusually rich with thrift stores. Some of this is because of the cultural shift: a profoundly strong middle class invests strongly in Middle Class Stuff. And then when that middle class falls on hard times, when it disintegrates, when it shrinks, some of that Middle Class Stuff is abandoned, to yard sales and thrift stores. It's a matter of human mathematics: after the long division, the remainder doesn't disappear. It has to go somewhere. Meanwhile, the hard times generate a clientele that needs thrift. And they also generate a clientele that recognizes the meaning of certain kinds of legacies. Bowling, for instance. So all those polyester shirts find their way to the Goodwill rack and so do the seekers, and the culture replenishes itself.

(I think it is no coincidence that Akron and Dacron are not just phonetic but aesthetic homonyms.)

By the time I started rifling through the cultural remains, thrift stores were operating at a high level of refinement, such that one understood the nuances between Goodwill, Salvation Army, and Amvets the same way Rodeo Drive sophisticates distinguish between Gucci, Armani, and Dior.

The store where Dave and I shopped was near the university, and hence its book selection was huge, and excellent. In the same way that I had begun to gravitate toward Grosset & Dunlap spines as a child, I now received a slight electric charge when I spotted one of the icons that represented a kind of taste that was emerging in my new, older self. The orange-and-white penguin, the Viking ship, the stylized flame. Based solely on imprint association, I discovered William Kennedy, Mary Gordon, Gabriel García Márquez.

It wasn't so much that these books matched my aesthetic. I didn't have one, not in any kind of evolved fashion. It was more that an aesthetic began to form amid the randomness and the seeking, and that these connections began to represent some kind of order. I was taking on the properties of my surroundings.

My strongest previous connection to the commercial center of the city was my family's annual visits to see the Christmas windows at the two big department stores, Polsky's and O'Neil's, which sat directly across Main Street from one another, five-story opposing façades positioned for a retail standoff. My two brothers and my sister and I would stand on the sidewalk, our breath fogging the plate glass as we peered at the jerky repetition of mechanized elves, steam rising around us from the manhole covers as my mother read the script verses describing the various scenes.

But now Polsky's had been closed for four years, and O'Neil's, deep in decline, had discontinued its displays and there wasn't much reason to go downtown. Akron's first suburban shopping mall had opened the year after I was born. My parents had a seven-inch promotional record with a snappy jingle and a driver's-ed filmstrip narrator championing the virtues of the department stores and the wide concourses and the safe, easy parking. Nobody was chirping for us to go downtown. Nobody was cutting records about anachronistic urban consumerism.

Despite that, or maybe because of it, the central city held something different for me and my peers—the promise of rummaging and cheap discovery. So that day when we went looking to outfit ourselves, Dave drove us there in his epically crappy, maroon Pontiac Astre and we approached the store full of hope and, well, goodwill. The long, low cinder-block building extended at one end into a loading dock. This was the main warehouse for drop-off and distribution, so the vast detritus of the community was sorted here and categorized and put on display.

We entered through the double glass doors. Before us were long racks packed densely with the ends of things and the beginnings of others, a tangible circular narrative with card-stock signs suspended from the ceiling as monuments to the various divisions: Men's Coats; Girls' Dresses; Small Appliances. The store was blankly lit with fluorescent tubes and steeped in a complex aroma. From within, it emanated the musty, piss-tinged acridity of used clothing and the occasionally hygiene-deficient clientele. But it also gathered the prominent sour-sweetness that meandered from the big Wonder-bread factory across the street, an institution at the edge of the University of Akron campus whose brick, like all of central Akron's brick, was darkened by years of carbon black from the tire-plant smokestacks.

In a city that had always been described by its smell, students at the university invariably defined their college experience by the scent of Wonder bread. But it didn't smell like bread. It smelled like bread *baking*. There's a difference. In a manufacturing city, the distinction was vital: the experience defined not by the product, but the making of the product.

Dave went off to the row of sport coats and I started sorting methodically through the men's shirts. As a result of my regular visits, I knew that a focused, systematic approach was the only way to find anything good. This was not a venue for browsing. Chance was not enough. You start at the beginning and you don't take the easy way out, and you stay that way until you've reached the end.

On November 6, 1995, one more in an incessant series of officially-bizarre-couldn't-happen-anywhere-else events involving northeast-Ohio sports happened. Cleveland Browns owner Art Modell announced that he was moving his football team to Baltimore. The region was stunned and outraged. An immediate surge of resistance began, from street level on up through the legal system. The eventual result was an equally bizarre compromise: Modell would keep his team (i.e., the players, administration, organization), but Cleveland would keep the Browns' name, colors, history, records, etc. In a region defined for the previous generation by an identity crisis, here was one we could really sink out teeth into—an empty suit.

A familiar plain brown uniform with nothing inside.

But as seems to be the common evolution of our upheavals, the story took on greater complexity in the thrift stores. At the same time Browns fans were clamoring to keep their beloved team name and colors in Ohio, they apparently were throwing away any item of clothing that bore that name and colors.

In the weeks and months following the announcement, I found the thrift-store racks dense with orange-and-brown team apparel. Sweatshirts, T-shirts, jerseys, pajama pants, satin jackets, ugly orange stocking caps with brown pom-poms on top. Nothing defines the jilted more than the wardrobe tossed with hurt and anger out the front door.

Get out and stay out, the thrift stores seemed to say, even as we were begging, *Please don't leave us.*

This, as much as anything, captures the paradox of a culture that loves something that offers heartache upon heartache in return.

And then, fifteen years later, another turn of the screws. LeBron James, who was supposed to deliver us from these miseries, announced that he was "taking his talents to South Beach." In a region pocked with the scars of sports infamy, this was the deepest cut we had ever known, perhaps ever could know. The other incidents—the Shot, the Drive, the Fumble, etc.—all stank of ill fate. But this one was different because the notion of fate stretched all the way from James's birth in Akron through his rise in prominence. After he was drafted by the Cavaliers in 2003, Nike signed him to a $90 million endorsement deal, and the shoe company created the famous "Witness" campaign with all its messianic overtones, including a line of T-shirts that represented a new uniform for the region.

Within weeks after "the Decision," I went to the Village Thrift, arguably the finest secondhand store in all of America. What I found was almost surreal. A density of black Witness T-shirts lining the racks, so many that it almost looked as if this were its own department. One of the ubiquitous television images in the immediate wake of James's announcement was of angry fans torching their LeBron gear. And while that purge was dramatic, it was nothing like what the racks of the thrift store announced. A complete disowning.

In addition to the Witness T-shirts, the racks were stocked with No. 23 jerseys and King James T-shirts and all other manner of clothing devoted to his brand. This display told the story perhaps even better than those video clips. Because the burning—that seemed spontaneous and extreme, a public spectacle. But the funneling of all those countless items of clothing, discarded not as some sort of organized protest, but rather a cascading identical private act, suggested something of our shared subconscious. We all, without needing to be told, knew what to do. To shed the tainted skin before it defined us.

We are well versed in this.

Dave had found what he was looking for, a brown sharkskin suit jacket that fit well enough. He approached me with it draped over his arm.

"Any luck?" he asked.

I shook my head and paused, my hands parting the wall of shirts. "Not yet."

He went down to the end of the rack where I'd begun, retracing my path through wrinkled polos and pit-stained dress shirts. I continued, locked in on the search, determined. I flipped through the hangered shirts mechanically, certain now of what I didn't want, which was a step closer to understanding what I did want. And then, deep into the line, I found one. A bowling shirt. I pulled it out. It was plain, barely adorned. Gray polyester, shapeless, more barber's frock than *New York Rocker,* with a wide collar that ended in long points. There was no team name across the back, just a simple black band around the bottom hem and at the end of each sleeve and across the top seam of the breast pocket. A name, not stitched but stamped, was in script appliqué above the pocket.

Dave.

Really?

My own name?

I wasn't sure what to make of that. Was it more ironic? Or was this fate, an announcement that the shirt was placed there special, just for me? Or was it a mockery—no one ever called me

Dave except for my older brother, but only when he was trying to taunt. Long before, in second grade, I'd started writing Dave on my school papers. When I received my official-membership card signifying me as a "member in good standing" of the G.I. Joe Adventure Team, I wrote *Dave Giffels* on the line for my name. I thought it sounded more grown-up, more debonair. But my mother soon took me aside and explained kindly but firmly that she and my father had chosen the name David carefully, and it meant "beloved," and I was not to defile it by shortening it to the familiar. So I was David. Yet the shirt offered to me by Goodwill suggested I was, in my new guise, to be Dave.

Or maybe fate hadn't even planted the shirt for me at all. Maybe it was meant for my friend there at the end of the rack, someone who actually went by Dave.

If the guiding coming-of-age question for the high school graduate (and the thrift-store seeker) is, "Who am I?" this shirt seemed to suggest an answer: "Approximately who you already are."

Hardly a definitive revelation, but time was short and I was near the end of the rack.

With my friend still trailing behind, I completed my search with no further success. This shirt would have to do. We made our purchases and headed back into the world.

WORKING HARD
OR HARDLY WORKING?

You really need to understand about the bowling. Nothing serves as a better cultural metaphor for the peak and dark valley of industrial America better than the game of tenpins. But not for the reasons you might think.

Bowling, to Akron, is something like sex to Paris and celebrity to Los Angeles and dry heat to Phoenix. It is the thing which informs the culture and that which the culture informs. It is language spoken back into the native mouth. All the plastic, gold trophies on display in the fellowship halls and the Chianti-bottle Italian joints are of men bent deeply forward, one arm extended, captured in the moment either of graceful release or of being yanked into their future by a dense, black sphere.

When you have a city built so directly on three things—industry, hierarchy, and polymer compounds—you are bound to have some serious bowling leagues. And Akron did. You look in the old-photo morgues and you find stacks and stacks of things like black-and-white glossies of company bowling teams with the men posed shoulder to shoulder, photos that neatly—uncannily—juxtapose with the portraits of Harvey S. Firestone's five blue-blooded sons, also standing shoulder to shoulder, and there's really no difference. Ultimately they are all heir to the same fortunes.

This idea of intense bowling activity was true everywhere in blue-collar middle-class America anytime in the postwar twentieth century. But in Akron, where the ideals of Work and Industry operated at such a level of high concept, the culture of bowling could not exist as a casual notion. It just couldn't. Akron has never done anything that way. Places like this are self-conscious, worried, busy, hardheaded, and diligent. These kinds of places leave nothing to luck. They are the opposite of cool, which is not necessarily a bad thing, but definitely is a necessary thing. In Akron, where bowling teams oozed from the tire factories like excess plastic from an extrusion, bowling had to be serious, otherwise it would seem counterproductive.

To correct this idea of bowling as a trivial pastime, Akron invented the Professional Bowlers Association. This ensured that the game would not be perceived as mere relaxation. Relaxation in heavily union towns can only be one of two things: a vice or a reward. As such, it needs to be done either in private or in Florida. Not in a bowling alley.

And that's how bowling, quintessential recreation of the middle class, was turned by Akron into a profession. In 1958 the Professional Bowlers Association (PBA) formed here and the notion of "organized bowling" became formalized. Firestone Tire & Rubber became the lead sponsor of the Tournament of Champions, the sport's Super Bowl, held in an Akron suburb.

Akron, seizing as it so often does on slim recognition, declared itself the Sports Capital of the World, a proclamation splashed across the frontispiece of the 1978 *Akron City Directory*, which offered the evidence of "famous events like the All-American Soap Box Derby, the National Skate-Board Championships, the World Series of Golf and the $150,000 Firestone Tournament of Champions bowling tournament."

Hyperbolic superlatives like this always seemed to be attached to my place, and I could never figure out how to process them. The Rubber Capital of the World also claimed to be the birthplace of the hamburger *and* the ice cream cone, and to have spawned the first American punk-rock club outside New York City. Cleveland, our next-door neighbor to the north, claimed to be the Rock and Roll Capital of the World. Canton, our next-door neighbor to the south, goes by the nickname Birthplace of Professional Football. As a teenager, I was fascinated by my hometown's reputation as pop music's "new Liverpool"—a designation sparked by the sudden popularity of the locally born Devo—and the widespread use of the term *Akron sound* to describe New Wave. When the Akron bands sought to capitalize on this attention, they collaborated to release a local compilation album and called it *Bowling Balls from Hell*.

Hamburgers and ice cream and bowling and rock music and soap-box racers and Chuck Taylors and football! And blimps!

Children! Why are you leaving here?

But I didn't know how to contextualize any of it. Either Akron was unusually culturally significant—special—or every place had its own version of this and was equally culturally significant, which would mean that my place was not special at all.

Just outside of Akron, off a two-lane highway that led into the neighboring town of Kent, was a bowling ball factory. It sat down in a valley, in concert with the river and the railroad tracks. It seemed exotic, but also entirely logical: We were a place that made things, by hand, from scratch, often with rugged ingenuity, like the Amish or the Little Rascals. We needed bowling balls and so we made them, there in that mysterious factory, a long whistle calling in the shift so that the men and the women could come in and craft sixteen-pound globes for the industrial leagues, some black, some neon, some fancy with swirls. I like to think that the factory workers themselves formed a company team, to bowl with the company balls, and that they were good, the best. That theirs was both the height and the justification of craft. Regardless of that desire, one truth stands clear. We were a closed loop. We completed our own synapses. It all made sense.

Until the night the factory blew up.

I don't know when it happened, maybe a long time before I heard about it, maybe two days before, but the legend was immediate and profound, of a night sky filled with an explosion of black spheres spewing in all directions, a confetti of cannonballs. Where did they land? Who found them? What destruction ensued? Was anyone killed? And what, then, was the logic in this?

I worked one summer with a guy named Keith. Keith liked his beer. We all knew that. Friday after work, he was gone, off to dollar-pitcher night somewhere or other. I was working that year on the dummy end of a surveying crew, and Keith was the sort of flawed icon who helps young men like me define what a man is. He was dark haired, rugged, and hardworking, fixed his own car, bitched about the government, wore combat boots and an army jacket and faded jeans, and he taught me how to steady a plumb bob over a nail head and also how to engage in the Banter of Guys. We spent our days hacking through brush with machetes, tanned and lean, waving our arms to shoo the bugs and pollen we'd disturbed, clearing sight lines to view the measuring rod once we'd located our corners, dragging a hundred-foot tape to measure the distances. We ate lunch and took water breaks in the hot metal shell of the company van, the air inside fragrant with the pine of property stakes and lath, the walls speckled with errant sprays of orange paint. That's the kind of work for which cold beer was invented as a reward. Beer was, for many generations of human society, served warm and heady. I like to think that it was an American man like Keith who deduced that, if thinned and chilled, beer would serve as the fittest reward for hot summer work and should therefore be offered at a discount price in the hours immediately following that work. That Keith himself invented happy hour. But even if he was not the originator, he was an avid practitioner.

And so one Monday morning he came into the office limping badly.

"What happened?" we asked him.

"Well," he said, "I went out to Kent after work on Friday and had me some beers. When I came out of the bar, it was still light out. And as I was walking up to the next bar, I saw a ball on the sidewalk, like a kid's dodgeball, and decided I was gonna kick it down to the river. So I backed up for a running start and laid into it. And it didn't *move*."

He looked at us a long moment.

"It was a bowling ball."

He limped for a long time until he got better, and he told the story more than once, and I could never tell if he was embarrassed or proud, but I now understand that he must have been proud, that this was his story to tell, and eventually I wished it were mine.

I don't know if these two legends are connected in fact, but I do know that they are forever connected in my mind, and I can no longer extract one from the other and I no longer want to. I want to believe that all this happened together, that the shift ended at the bowling ball factory on a Thursday night, that everyone went home, that a stray, random spark found purchase in something powerful, powerful enough to do the job completely, and that the explosion sent those countless balls into a pattern of chaos, but one landed there on the sidewalk near the bar and lay there till the next evening, waiting with predetermination for Keith to get just tight enough to come outside, a grown man feeling as if the world still holds its possibilities for him, despite the day-after-day-after-days inside the hot company van, that joy and surprise and inspiration always exist and always will and—there, just like that!—in his path was proof, and when he gave himself over to the act, fully, completely, and his foot struck nothing but the dense urethane of resistance, that nothing changed, that despite the pain, the disillusion, the bitter folly, that for all that, the bowling ball was an even better surprise. That right there in the hurt where the boot met the ball: proof there was meaning in this.

There should be a gold, plastic trophy for guys like that.

For decades, the PBA was housed in a strip mall in Akron, a world headquarters that, for better or for worse, represented a prime tentacle of our public image. Akron, for much of my life, was intimately associated with the least fashionable of all professional sports, fraught with mullets and polyester slacks and chicken-shack physiques and mustaches that made the whole thing resemble a porn shoot at a Walmart. We sat some Saturday afternoons watching the Tournament of Champions on national television, thrilled that the event was taking place at the same nearby bowling alley where my dad's beer league played once a week.

Both despite and because of its proletarian association, the presence of professional bowling's world headquarters a couple of miles from my home—tucked in between a drive-through convenience store and a health club—seemed exotic and important. Another one of those "We Are Here!" declarations that we shouted with increasing urgency. Like so many other of these touchstones, that we had created the entity and continued to foster it within our community was a source of great meaning. Akron was bowling, and bowling was Akron. These are cities that make things, and whether those things are lug nuts or philosophical entities, their role is profoundly important.

Therefore, in 2000, when a group of former Microsoft executives bought the PBA and unceremoniously uprooted it from its Akron foundation, the hurt was as deep as it was familiar. The purchase and removal of our major institutions had been the story of the previous decade. The French company Michelin had bought Goodrich and moved the headquarters to Greenville, South Carolina. The Japanese company Bridgestone had bought Firestone and moved the headquarters to Nashville. The German company Continental had bought General and moved the headquarters to Charlotte. Even the locally born international union followed this path, as the United Rubber Workers merged with the much larger United Steelworkers, which moved the headquarters to Pittsburgh.

So off to Seattle went professional bowling.

When you stay in a place like this and watch people and ideas and institutions leave and you trace the patterns and the imbalances, that becomes part of your generation's definition, and then it becomes a matter of identity and pride, replacing the old versions, and begging for a new definition.

I stay in a place that people leave.

CUTTING THE MUSTARD

So I'm standing around one day, talking to a friend from out of state, and I casually mention that Akron is the birthplace of the hamburger, and he stops cold and gives me one of those cartoon, you're-out-of-your-gourd looks.

"The birthplace of the hamburger?" he says. "That's like saying corn was invented in Nebraska."

But of course Akron is the home of the hamburger. Just as it is the Rubber Capital of the World, Blimp City, and the Sports Capital of the World—all nicknames the city has adopted at one time or another, all in the realm of the superlative. This is important, an odd matter of psychological balance.

To celebrate this heady claim and to explore both its capacity and that of my colon, I decided by the end of that conversation that I would embark on a spiritual journey. I would spend one solid week eating nothing but my city's famous hamburgers.

No vegetables, save for some wrinkled pickle slices and greasy mushrooms. No fruit, except, in a moment of weakness, a slice of apple pie at an old workingman's diner. I gulped down a couple gallons of root beer and ate enough french fries to stabilize Idaho's economy.

I ate wide burgers and tall burgers and square burgers and sliders. I ate carhop burgers as if I were a member of Sha Na Na. I tried to eat a burger at one of those ritzy blue-hair steak houses that people like me only go to on prom dates, but they wouldn't serve me one.

After a while, it all started to become a tangled puzzle. If the Ido Bar & Grill serves the Famous Ido Burger, what to make of Bob's Hamburg's claim Famous Since 1931, and the Main Street Saloon's Famous Jumbo Burger?

In a celebrity age, when everyone with a Twitter following has a kind of virtual renown, what does "famous" even mean?

Where is the truth?

I began on a Monday. Recognizing that the high-concept purposeful consumption of a single food category has become something of a journalistic subgenrc, I followed the example of my forebears, stopping for a visit with a nurse to chart my baseline vitals. One hundred fifty and three-quarter pounds of red-blooded American carnivore. My blood pressure was normal, 112 over 74. Although all that beef was likely to affect my cholesterol level, she said it wouldn't show up for months, so we didn't bother measuring for that. Besides, I didn't want to know.

And so I was off.

For seven days, I would be asked the same philosophical question over and over: "Want fries with that?"

Damn straight I do.

My quest began at Menches Bros., a restaurant owned by a family that clings proudly to its claim that its ancestors invented the hamburger. (And the ice-cream cone and Cracker Jack. But that's another story.)

As the legend goes, Frank and Charles Menches, wealthy businessmen from Akron, happened along their invention by accident. They were making their living as fair vendors, hauling a tent around on a train car and selling food. One day in 1885 (or 1892, depending on the iteration of the story), while working the local county fair (or, in some iterations, a fair in New York), they ran short of sausages. They called on a local meat vendor, who told them he had no sausage links, only ground sausage.

"We've got to have sandwich meat," Frank Menches recalled in a 1938 newspaper interview. "Send over that tub of ground sausage!"

The industrious brothers formed the sausage into patties, fried it up, and the sandwiches sold like, uh, hotcakes. So the next day, when it came time to buy their meat, they decided to save a little money and make beef sandwiches—the butcher was charging 4¢ a pound more for sausage.

Frank Menches said he told the butcher to run some beef through the grinder. It came out "just dandy," he said, and he and his brother sold about a thousand pounds of beef patties each day of the fair. They didn't have a name yet, so they just hollered, "Get your hot sandwiches here!"

Two years later, according to the story, they discovered another vendor at an Ohio fair selling the same ground-beef sandwiches, calling them hamburgers. They adopted the name, and "everybody's called 'em hamburgers ever since," Frank said.

Fast-forward to 1991, the Menches family reunion. Some of the adults got to talking and decided to sell some old-style Menches burgers at the county fair later that summer. They were a hit, and in 1994, five of Charles Menches's great-grandchildren got together and opened Menches Bros. restaurant.

Judy Menches-Kusmits has become the family historian, carefully pulling together evidence to strengthen the family's claim as the unmoved mover of the hamburger. There are some problems with that, chiefly that the 1938 newspaper story says the invention happened in 1892.

Menches-Kusmits insists it was 1885. The source she uses to back up the family's claim, a book called *Tanbark and Tinsel*, differs from the newspaper story in a number of details. There, the author, who also relies on an interview with Frank Menches, writes that the sandwich was concocted at New York's Erie County Fair, held in the city of Hamburg.

The 1885 date is important because of a place called Seymour, Wisconsin, the self-proclaimed Home of the Hamburger.

Every year at the beginning of August, Seymour celebrates its Burger Fest. They have a parade with hamburger floats. They have a hamburger-stacking contest. They have a Hamburger King and Queen. They have a rather disturbing-sounding event that involves small children sliding in ketchup.

They take their hamburgers seriously up there in Seymour.

In 1988, the town of three thousand barbecued its way into the *Guinness Book of World Records* with a 5,525-pound hamburger. It was twenty-one feet across—the size of a two-car garage, as they proudly note. Thirteen thousand people ate from it, and there was still enough left to donate to a food bank.

Their festival celebrates the legacy of a man named Charlie Nagreen—the founder of the hamburger.

Vivian Treml, president of Home of the Hamburger, the group that runs the Burger Fest and the local Hamburger Hall of Fame, told me the story: It was 1885. Hamburger Charlie, as he has come to be known, was a fifteen-year-old fair vendor, hauling around a load of meatballs in a wagon pulled by a team of oxen. The meatballs weren't going over too well with fairgoers looking for finger food, so he flattened them, slapped them between two pieces of bread, and called them hamburgers. They sold like, uh, hotcakes. Yes, I thought the story sounded familiar, too. But it seems unfair (and perhaps unwise) to suggest the notion of myth to a town whose pride hinges on a two-and-a-half-ton hamburger.

Our two towns are not alone. Hamburg, New York; Athens, Texas; and New Haven, Connecticut, also claim to be the birthplace of the American hamburger. *Encyclopaedia Britannica* says the real origin of the sandwich is unknown, but it was probably brought to the United States by nineteenth-century German immigrants, whose chopped-beef sandwich was named for the city of Hamburg.

As I sat in Menches Bros. talking to Judy Menches-Kusmits, she showed me some books about the history of hamburgers. Those that deal with the dueling claimants don't state definitively who gets credit for the invention, but the Menches family is sticking to its guns. So is Seymour.

We talked awhile. I told Judy I was planning to eat nothing but hamburgers for a week.

This woman, to whom the hamburger is as important as her own family, looked me dead in the eye and said, "You're not really going to do that."

Yes, Judy, I am.

Did you ever notice how, when you stare at a hamburger, it looks as if it were smiling at you? Okay, maybe that's just me. But it's such a friendly American icon. The round-topped sandwich with the slice of beef peeking out is so familiar. It's the Wilford Brimley of sandwiches.

I love those big plastic guys that stand outside Big Boy, holding the big plastic hamburger on the big plastic tray. I remember the news stories a while back when one got stolen from the front of a restaurant in suburban Ohio, how the manager said plaintively, "We miss the big fella."

I tried to explain some of this to my four-year-old son as we sat waiting for our hamburgers at a carhop place in Akron. I pointed to the Soap Box Derby track right across the road, told him how kids raised on hamburgers race homemade cars down that hill. I pointed over to the Rubber Bowl, the University of Akron's football field, and told him John Heisman used to coach there, and now his name is on the trophy given to the best college football player in America. I pointed over to the giant old Goodyear Airdock, told him how zeppelins used to fly out of there, how *Ripley's Believe It or Not* called it one of the wonders of the world.

I told him we live in an important place. I think I even said "mythical."

I could smell the hamburgers cooking inside the little kitchen and was moved to ask the question that is not really a question:

"Did you know the hamburger was invented in Akron?"

He looked me straight in the eye and responded with the four-year-old's version of "That's like saying corn was invented in Nebraska."

Bob's Hamburg is a shrine to the great American sandwich, a cramped, old-style diner with red vinyl stools at the Formica counter and Patsy Cline on the jukebox. A tiny nook in the corner is called the Bahama Room. It can seat six, if they like each other a lot.

A McDonald's opened across the street from Bob's in the 1960s, a seeming death knell to the little mom-and-pop. The McDonald's went out of business in 1997. Bob's did not.

A man and a woman were discussing their bowling scores in the next booth as the waitress asked me what I wanted.

"Hamburger," I said.

Barb Schlagenhauser, the owner, stopped by after a while. My hamburger was smiling at me as Barb told me a little about the history of the place. As the sign declares, it has been famous since 1931, when Bob Holbrook first opened the doors. But most people know it as the domain of a man named Walt Ridge, who owned it from 1934 until his death in 1981.

"He had a heart attack there in the Bahama Room," Barb said wistfully.

She introduced me to another customer, an old regular who'd come this day to celebrate his seventy-sixth birthday. He has been a regular here for most of his life, he said, grew up around the corner.

"People say, 'Where you goin' to lunch?'" he said, then offered his answer as though they'd asked the color of the sky: "Bob's."

Barb sells a couple hundred hamburgers a day. That's what she does—she watches people eat hamburgers.

But when I told her about my special diet, she made a bad face and said, "Oh, *Gawd!*"

The valet approaches. A valet is kind of like a carhop, except a carhop brings you food and a valet takes your car.

I am wearing a tie and a linen suit, practicing in my head exactly how I am going to order a hamburger in the only restaurant in Akron I could think of where it would seem ridiculous to order a hamburger.

I try it with an English accent. "I'd like an om-burga, my good man." Maybe?

The lighting is dim, the music sublime. The waiters are in tuxedos. People are drinking martinis from wide glasses and eating expensive steaks and influencing Republican politics. The grill chef works behind a brick half-wall in the dining room. I shoot a glance in his direction as the maître d' ushers my wife and me through the dining room. I don't see any ground beef, anywhere.

We start with an appetizer of oysters Rockefeller, a canny tactic to throw the waiter off the scent. Nice people out for a classy dinner, he must be thinking. I like the cut of their jib. Nice tie on that guy, too.

I consider my order again. Righteous indignation? Maybe that's it. *What do you mean there are no hamburgers on the menu? What kind of place is this?*

The waiter approaches. My wife orders filet and scampi.

He turns to me. "And for the gentleman?"

"I'd like a hamburger," I say, my Akron twang hanging out like a street cleaner's shirttail.

He appears more than slightly concerned. "I don't think we can do that," he says drily.

"Couldn't the chef just chop up a filet?" I say, making the international meat-cleaver motion with my hand.

"I can ask," he says, his forehead creasing.

The waiter leaves, huddles with a few others over by the grill chef.

He returns. "I'm sorry. We can't make you a hamburger. And"—pausing for effect, leaning in closer—"that's straight from the owner."

I try to look disappointed, but I realize that, at this very moment, I am being given a reprieve—straight from the owner!—from my carnal incarceration. I want to rip the menu from his hands and scan it for the diametrical opposite of a hamburger. I want vegetables! I want fresh fruit! I want poached fish! Pasta! Soup!

I order a steak.

I decided to end this thing in the American way, with a Sunday-evening barbecue. Me, fire, cow meat.

I stared at the glowing embers in my grill.

We all need to be somebody, I thought. That's why every humble place in America has one of those signs at the city limits that says WELCOME TO (YOUR MUNICIPALITY HERE), HOME OF (CLAIM TO FAME HERE).

I understand Seymour, with its garage-size hamburger, wanting to cling to its pride. But, Seymour, you've got to understand. We were somebody once. We were a lot of things. We kind of need something to remain our own.

One by one, I dropped the patties onto the grill. In a short time, I will have eaten my last hamburger. I will find, at my weigh-in the next day, that I have gained only one pound and my blood pressure has barely budged. I will find that I have survived, future cholesterol results be damned. I will remember every hamburger fondly, the nights we shared, their smiling faces.

I will say, Thank you, Akron. Thank you for the hamburgers.

I will gladly pay you Tuesday.

HOUSEROCKERS

"Rock and roll will either kill ya, or it'll keep you young."

Michael Stanley made this breathy proclamation as I was interviewing him over the telephone one afternoon in the early 1990s. The middle-aged host of a local light-features television program called *Cleveland Tonight*, Stanley had recently suffered a heart attack. A longtime smoker, he seemed to have misinterpreted his current state, which was something in between dead and young.

It is likely you don't think of Michael Stanley as a television host. It is far more likely that you think of him either as a major rock star or as someone you've never heard of and don't think of at all. This paradox is everything.

He said those words with such conviction that for a moment they seemed true, undeniable, wise even, especially to someone like me, for whom rock and roll is a central obsession and who at the time was a relatively young man and prone to think in such broad, anthemic terms. (Confession: I wrote a poem when I heard that Shannon Hoon had died. And I didn't even like Blind Melon.)

So—yes. Rock and roll is both a destructive force and a vital one. Witness please the martyrdom of Kurt Cobain and Mama Cass Elliot and Pigpen McKernan and also the way it has kept Bob Dylan and Joan Baez and Rod Stewart forever young. There is no in between.

But this notion dissolved quickly, as did my ability to believe it. Michael Stanley is the quintessential "hometown hero" rock musician, a workingman singer-songwriter who almost broke through three decades ago and has remained comfortably nestled in Cleveland, lionized by his neighbors ever since. Just about every major city in the industrial East and Midwest has its own version of this.

In Cleveland, it's Michael Stanley. Buffalo has Willie Nile. Pittsburgh has two: Donnie Iris and Joe Grushecky. The workingman towns along the Jersey shore have Southside Johnny. (Detroit's version, Bob Seger, actually is famous well beyond his hometown, but this makes him the exception that proves the rule and also reinforces the grand scale of Detroit's Rust Beltedness.)

Stanley has been delivering such messages to a faithful audience for decades. His words strike me now as charmingly extreme, the sort of wishful absolutism that congeals in the mind of a certain type of working-class, Midwestern rock songwriter for whom the anthem is the pinnacle of expression. And a rock anthem, by commercial necessity, cannot afford the weight of ambiguity. Every rose has a fucking thorn, goddamnit, and that's just the way it is. It must be so. This is how life can make sense.

Love: is like a rock.

This town: is my town.

I was born in a small town: I'm gonna die in a small town.

I rock: therefore I am.

The rise of the regional "heartland rocker" happened, not coincidentally, at the same time as the decline of the industrial revolution, in the 1980s, as factory cities in the East and Midwest began their crises of economy and identity. Our cities embodied a kind of reality-based myth about hard work and simple values and denim-as-metaphor, and so if we were to have bards, we needed them to be the sort that we could sip cold proletarian beer to, and who would reward us with notions of escape (usually via muscle car) and loyalty (my daddy worked in the factory) and romance (bleached video blonde who listens attentively to the guitar solo). Country music did not yet have these markets cornered.

Uniquely, then, and with remarkable conformity, the major cities of this region each manufactured its own golem of the midshelf rock and roller in a fashion that seemed at once organic and prefabricated.

In each instance, the bandleader's name was the name of his band:

The Michael Stanley Band. Donnie Iris and the Cruisers. Joe Grushecky and the Houserockers (adapted from the name of his first band, one of the best rock-band names ever: the Iron City Houserockers). Willie Nile. Southside Johnny and the Asbury Jukes.

Each of them has been called, at some point, "the Springsteen of (Your City Here)." The comparison is unavoidable, and the convention is resoundingly consistent: an earnest male, Telecaster-playing, dark-haired Caucasian leading a local bar band that flirted in some way with national fame, never quite made it to the big time, but remained, and remains, a regional icon. As time has passed, each of these figures has come to occupy the territory between the frustration of what might have been and the comfort of knowing they will always be loved and financially supported by the audiences that were pulling for them in the first place. They dress in blue jeans and loose-cut blazers, bravely holding a middle ground between the anxieties of art and unconcerned artlessness. Where once they represented working-class rock and roll, they are now gainfully employed middle-class rockers, with careers that mirror actual careers in plumbing and auto sales; they have a clientele and know the tricks of their trade and are fully vested in their retirement plans.

The proof of a real-life stereotype comes when a fictional version can easily be drawn. Witness then *Eddie and the Cruisers*, a film (based, it's worth mentioning, on a novel by an Ohioan, P. F. Kluge) whose basic story is that of any of the musicians mentioned above. Gritty, heartfelt rock band with working-class hopes and dreams flirts with industry success only to hit the skids. The stereotype transcends when the fiction results in a furthering of the founding presumption. Therefore, when the New England bar band John Cafferty and the Beaver Brown Band was enlisted to compose some of the music for the sound track, the group's saxophone player was such a dead ringer for his scripted counterpart that the director cast him in the film, as the Cruisers' sax man. There was no way to differentiate between life and art.

So of course Michael Stanley believes that rock and roll will either kill ya or keep you young. It's his profession of faith, and his faith has delivered the unlikeliest profession.

Proclamations such as these thrive in the geometric efficiency of the four-chord rock song. Not three (although the three-chord song would not be out of place in this territory). And definitely not five. Too ostentatious. Four is the sweet spot.

The four-chord riff has a distinct place in pop rock, and a subtle yet revealing aesthetic. If you looked at, say, the pop charts of 1982—a galvanizing year for the Industrial Belt and its six-string composers—you could trace the entire scope of the musical culture by measuring the patterns of the main riff:

"Jessie's Girl" (Rick Springfield, four chords) = the mild complexity of this emotional situation will be defined thusly in the following three verses and intervening choruses, with a satisfying resolution.

"I Love Rock 'n' Roll" (Joan Jett and the Blackhearts, three chords) = for the following two minutes and fifty-four seconds I will express my strong affinity for rock and roll.

"Should I Stay or Should I Go" (the Clash, two chords) = here we shall parse the dualized horns of a Frostian dilemma, only with Paul Simonon on bass.

"We Got the Beat" (the Go-Go's, one chord) = we have another one but we'll be using it in the next song.

"Eminence Front" (the Who, no chords) = not even trying at this point.

As I said, the four-chord rock riff is the sweet spot of the working-class bar anthem, in the way it hits the launching pad of its come-around chord and then leaps into the open arms of the chorus. Think of the great American (okay, Canadian) song of the working life, Bachman-Turner Overdrive's "Takin' Care of Business." If you can think of a more symmetrically satisfying song, please let me know.

A song like this is two parts meat and two parts potato. In the best of them, the chords are palm-muted in the verses, then fired open for the chorus. Middle bridge, guitar (or occasionally sax) solo, and then down the home stretch. It is a can't-miss approach, and frankly if you can't feel good hearing a song like that, well, I think that you think too much.

Youngstown is really good to me.
—DONNIE IRIS

So. Michael Stanley. Good-looking fellow, but not movie-star handsome. Beard, average build. Plays a Telecaster. Slightly rough-edged baritone. Emotions are handled with professionalism. Knows how to play to the back row.

You could post his picture next to *Wikipedia*'s definition of heartland rock: "a predominately romantic genre, celebrating 'urban backstreets and rooftops,' [whose] major themes have been listed as including 'unemployment, small-town decline, disillusionment, limited opportunity and bitter nostalgia,' as well as alienation and despair."

From "Midwest Midnight"
Take me back to Midwest midnight
Ten thousand watts of holy light from my radio so clear . . .

The whole lot of them—Stanley, Grushecky, Johnny, Willie, Donnie—came of age in the mid-1970s, peaked commercially in the early 1980s, and then began their real careers with a longevity that seems to be based as much on their local audiences' unfulfilled need for a winner as any music industry convention. Here is a case where the audience may need the artist even more than the artist needs the audience.

When I was first coming into an understanding of rock music, I just assumed that Michael Stanley and Bruce Springsteen were equally huge rock stars. At that moment, within my provincial limitations, they were. Both of them sold out the big area stadium venues. Both of their tour T-shirts were as ubiquitous around this part of Ohio as Browns jerseys. They coexisted as a sort of Apollo and Zeus of WMMS, the local mainstream FM rock powerhouse.

Bruce Springsteen, of course, was actively becoming the biggest rock icon in the world. But at the same time Springsteen was exploring his interior darkness with the lo-fi *Nebraska*, the Michael Stanley Band played four consecutive nights at Blossom Music Center, the big outdoor shed near Cleveland, and drew nearly seventy-five thousand fans. Stanley's song "My Town," with its "This town! Is my town!" fist-pump chorus, was the region's unofficial theme. It was a much bigger deal than "Hungry Heart," and I doubt even the Boss could have pulled off a four-night, packed-house residency.

But what I didn't recognize—what I couldn't recognize because of the way the media was manipulating this information and because I didn't have access to long-distance transportation and therefore the outer world—was that beyond the borders of greater Cleveland, Michael Stanley was barely on the radar. One song had scratched into the lower reaches of the *Billboard* Top 40 pop chart, "He Can't Love You," reaching No. 33. In Chicago, say, or Denver or Tallahassee, the Michael Stanley Band may as well have been Chilliwack.

But that didn't matter. As long as he stayed close to home, he would be needed and adored. It becomes a matter of self-fulfillment: as long as the local audience continues to support the musician, the musician appears to be as popular as the audience needs him to be for its own validation.

To this very day, Stanley, who now works as a drive-time DJ on the local classic-rock station and releases albums regularly, has a specific brand of iconic status, and a specific brand of deeply committed loyalty that is as admirable as it is hard to calculate.

In 2012, as I write this, Michael Stanley has recently played four consecutive weekend nights, sold-out shows, at an Akron cabaret-style dinner club called the Tangier. Those are the only concert dates listed on his website.

On a recent visit to Pittsburgh, I saw placards advertising an upcoming appearance by Donnie Iris and the Cruisers at the local Hard Rock Café. All the shows listed on the official Donnie Iris website were in or around Pittsburgh, except two—one in Cleveland and the other in Phoenix—at a "Steeler Fanfest" party the night before a football game between the Arizona Cardinals and the Pittsburgh Steelers. A home away from home.

Joe Grushecky and the Houserockers had thirteen summer concert dates listed on their website in 2012. Twelve were in the Pittsburgh area. The other was at a club on the Jersey shore, but interestingly, in a Freudian slip of a typo, the location was listed as "Asbury Park, PA."

Southside Johnny, the highest profile of the bunch, does well in Europe, but keeps close to the New Jersey region here in the States—New York, Atlantic City, Asbury Park. (The farthest US concert from home in 2012? Cleveland.)

> Rock 'n' roll should be made by truck drivers from Tupelo,
>   Mississippi.
> —SOUTHSIDE JOHNNY

I hated the Michael Stanley Band. I hated Bruce Springsteen. I hated the Doors. I hated Led Zeppelin. I hated this music for the three worst possible reasons:

1. Because I didn't like the people who liked that music.
2. Because, due to misguided antifashion snobbery, I had never really listened to it.
3. Because of my mother.

That third thing, the mother part, probably stemmed more from Charles Manson than anything else. She was genuinely afraid of hippies, and even though she was of the prime demographic to be a first-generation Beatles fan and therefore provide a proper foundation for my own musical taste, she, for a crucial time in my development, disavowed all rock music. (Sadly, her cultural stance softened just as disco and John Denver were emerging. Those were difficult years.)

So I actually wanted a rock and roll of absolutes—a music that would either kill me or make me young—but that wasn't possible. If I had just been given the Beatles, I could have found the Stones, and then I'd probably have made it safely to the Stooges. Instead, while I loved rock music, I found it constantly frustrating.

I could find occasional copies of *Maximumrocknroll,* but I could never find the records that were reviewed there. When I tried guitar, my fingers fell apart half through the two-chord pattern of "You Really Got Me." The longer my hair got, the less it looked like Tommy Stinson's. There was an ideal, but I couldn't find it anywhere I looked. I was getting my information in the wrong order, without context.

The first friend I had who had a car owned just two cassettes: the first Pretenders album and the Tubes' *Completion Backward Principle.* With a considerable void to negotiate, we relied mainly on MTV to fill it. It was all random; we had no guide and no evolved sense of quality. Briefly, we believed Lee Ritenour was New Wave because he wore tight, red pants and his video followed one by Split Enz, who we thought were definitely New Wave, but could also maybe have been rockabilly on account of their tremendous pompadours. A friend once admitted that he was sometimes confused about what was punk and what was New Wave—specifically, he thought the song "Rock the Casbah" was definitely New Wave because it included a synthesizer, even though the Clash probably qualified as punk. We made fun of him mainly to deflect the truth: we didn't have any more of a clue than he did. Then when I did find Springsteen and Zeppelin on my own terms, it was too late for it to be as pure and absolute as it would have been at seventeen.

If rock and roll were simple, life would be so much easier.

TRAPPED IN A WORLD
THAT THEY NEVER MADE

I discovered rock and roll in a decommissioned bank building, fiddling with a plastic cup of pale beer, dressed in another man's bowling shirt, and wishing I had the tricolor, flat-bottomed shoes that would grant me my transcendence.

I sat at a sticky table in the abandoned remains of a once-opulent savings and loan, feeling both inferior and exotic. Above me was a commanding balcony. Behind me was a vault with a big, complicated gold handle that looked like the steering wheel from the *Poseidon*. Passing by, asking for a light, was a scrawny young man with a Mohawk, whose request was clearly intended as an insult, but one I couldn't interpret.

We had been coming here for months, a few friends and I, sneaking in underage, although I suppose it isn't technically sneaking when no one cares. I'd been arriving most nights with my brother Ralph, who was old enough to get in. He would show the doorman his driver's license and I would follow right behind, flashing Ralph's college ID. Same picture, same name. A few times through and the doorman didn't even bother checking anymore.

We'd come this night to see the Generics, a rock band from my high school that was led by my friend John Puglia. The group had originally begun as a gag for a school talent show, Four Neat Guys, dressed in leisure suits and lip-synching to a record by the Tarriers, a B-level, 1950s folk group. Then someone decided to try it with instruments and play Clash and Who covers, even though only one of them could actually play—and he really could play, a trained guitarist who could reproduce Rush and .38 Special songs exactly as they sounded on the radio, impressing us all. Except in the Generics he didn't play guitar. He was the drummer. So there was a singer who wasn't a singer, some guitarists who weren't guitarists, and a drummer who was a guitarist but was not. Together, onstage, despite their real selves.

The Generics were preparing to go on, arranging amplifiers, plugging things in, adjusting pieces of the drum kit. The place was crowded, a mix of our high school friends and the Bank regulars, slightly older, slightly better versed in rock-and-roll convention. They had the right bowling shirts. They had stripes. They had spandex. They had Mohawks.

John had made a brilliant and audacious move toward that direction, having purchased a pair of shiny black leather Beatle boots by mail order from Trash & Vaudeville in Greenwich Village. We all shopped at the thrift stores, looking for such items, but none of us had ever taken such an audacious step as to go directly to the fountainhead and spend that kind of money. Fifty-nine dollars! For a pair of pointy-toed boots! From New York City! John, therefore, had attained a kind of elevated legitimacy. Except that in the brief time since he had begun wearing the boots, the nuances of cool had taken a turn from skinny ties and pointy boots to something less refined, more guttural and torn.

In response, John had covered the boots in aluminum foil and speckled them with spray paint. This completed an outfit that consisted of skinny, black jeans with a bandanna tied around the ankle, a sleeveless T-shirt printed with a hyperreal photograph of goldfish, and a porkpie hat. It's hard to say whether his fashion fit with the rest of the band because each of them looked as if he belonged in a separate group—and not just musical group, but demographic group. The guitar player was wearing a business suit. The bass player was wearing a necktie around his forehead like a kamikaze headband. And the drummer, who was a defensive lineman by day, wore his green football jersey with a chunky 65 across the front.

The Bank had retained most of the character of its former financial-institution self, such that the liquor was stored behind the ornate, round steel door of the old vault, and the president's office upstairs still had its mahogany paneling, and that's where people sometimes smoked pot, which I never quite understood, because I didn't think illegal things were done in public. But the biggest falsehood of its current incarnation was its size. For a rock club, it was huge. I had no context for this then, but would later understand that local bands simply didn't play in rooms that large. (In addition to its floor space, the Bank had a two-story-high ceiling, all of which made it a sonic nightmare. Someone had draped a parachute from the ceiling in an attempt to deaden the sound, but it didn't work. Drummers had to time their beats so they'd be playing off their own rhythm, rather than the echo of themselves, all of which would sound like an overwrought Brian Eno studio technique if it weren't so woefully unintentional.)

The club was attached to a hotel called the Hotel Anthony Wayne, which used to have a stately velvet lobby and five-star rooms. It had slowly descended into a transient hotel, and now its rooms were rented by the night to gutter drunks and crazy people. Its lit sign malfunctioned so that it looked as if the place were called the Hony Wayne, which seemed about right.

The most profound truth of the Bank was how dramatically it represented the collapse of the prevailing culture, a major downtown financial institution overtaken by punk rock, right there square in the middle of Main Street. And there were dozens and dozens of other examples—theaters, bowling alleys, churches, warehouses. Some people might have found that sad. I never did. I always found it thrilling, this notion of decadence and of abandon and of availability and of possibility. There's a quote I love, by the composer Ned Rorem (by way of Jonathan Lethem's *The Ecstasy of Influence*)—"Inspiration could be called inhaling the memory of an act never experienced."

That's exactly how I felt there, then.

The house music stopped and the Generics began. Because they knew only four chords, they chose covers to suit their limitations, playing "Clash City Rockers" right after "I Can't Explain," the former having exactly the same choppy rhythm and progression—E-D-A-E—except with a G tucked in the middle to avoid wholesale plagiarism. They had one original, called "Twirl Around," which used the same chords in a different order.

They played "Clampdown" and "Death or Glory" and "I Fought the Law." Having overmined the Clash catalog, they turned to the Sex Pistols' "Anarchy in the UK" and, oddly, "Downtown" by Petula Clark. I didn't know in any critical way whether they were good, but I knew for sure they were amazing, simply because they were doing *something*, doing *this*, right there, live, on a stage that may as well have been in the middle of Shea Stadium. John was a catalyst—that was his true talent—and the dance floor immediately was full and frenzied. Somehow he lost his shirt, and then, as the set reached its climax, he pulled out a guitar and strapped it on, a guitar with one string, not plugged into anything. At the end of the song, he smashed it, which might have elevated him into some godlike status had I not seen him do this every single time they'd played, including once in the school cafeteria and even once in practice, and watched him methodically hammer the thing back together in preparation for the next show.

We had happened into what seemed like a uniquely strange moment, but which now I understand was the only way such moments can occur in cities like mine: strangely.

Cleveland and Akron, through a combination of bizarre misunderstandings and ham-fisted manipulation, had become, momentarily, a focal point of American pop music.

A term had emerged in the international music press—*the Akron Sound*—and it wasn't intended to be ironic.

It stemmed from the large number of like-minded artists and musicians who had just recently departed Akron on their way to illogical mainstream success. A half-decade progression of notoriety unfolded like this:

Chrissie Hynde, an Akron native, had moved to London, wandered more or less by chance into the midst of the burgeoning punk scene, formed the Pretenders, and become a major rock star. Her mother learned of this when she was at the local mall one day and saw her daughter's picture on the cover of *NME*.

Devo, which had begun as a local band at a dinky club that predated the Bank, had departed for Los Angeles and scored a *Billboard* No. 14 hit with "Whip It," which still stands as the quintessential New Wave pop song.

The Waitresses, a locally formed offshoot of a band called Tin Huey, had an MTV hit—"I Know What Boys Like"—and played the theme song to my favorite TV show, *Square Pegs*.

Rachel Sweet, whose brother was our paperboy (yes, we cling to these connections), had sung "Everlasting Love" as a duet with teen idol Rex Smith; it was all over the radio.

The Cramps' singer, Lux Interior, was from Akron. Robert Quine, the guitarist for Richard Hell and the Voidoids and Lou Reed, was from here too. The director Jim Jarmusch, an Akronite who'd moved to New York and had a strong connection to the music scene, was getting lots of attention for his first film, *Permanent Vacation*, and was about to be awarded the Camera d'Or for *Stranger Than Paradise* at the Cannes Film Festival.

All of them had come from here. In addition, the Bank's most popular draw, a gritty power-pop band called Hammer Damage, had lost its lead guitarist to the Dead Boys, the freaking *Dead Boys*! In the hipster underground, the Akron celebrity-association meter went haywire.

In the midst of this, an interviewer in England asked Mark Mothersbaugh, the Devo front man, what Akron was like. "It's a lot like Liverpool," he responded, referring to the dingy industrial vibe. But the quote was misinterpreted to mean "musical hotbed." Before long, London-based Stiff Records released an album called *The Akron Compilation*, which included a scratch-'n'-sniff cover that smelled like rubber.

Meanwhile, as Akron was becoming identified with adventurous, mold-breaking new music, Cleveland, driven mainly by the mainstream AOR, behemoth rock station WMMS, had declared itself the Rock and Roll Capital of the World, a wild hyperbole that was accepted by the populous as gospel.

Regardless of the catchphrases and the hype, these *were* great rock-and-roll cities, and not just Akron and Cleveland, but Detroit and Minneapolis and Chicago and Youngstown and lots of places in between. This reflected not an inherent coolness, but rather more like the opposite, something bred in the nature of our existence. Rock and roll needs a void, and we had that, in abundance. We had empty garages and basements and warehouses, and great stretches of empty time, and—most important—no one paying attention.

Few bands in pop music history have been as calculated and inventive as Devo. But Devo spent years fucking around, sorting and sorting through the junk surrounding them to assemble their creation, writing manifestos, and developing broad personas. If Akron is a place that does things the hard way on purpose, then Devo could be our patron saint. They couldn't have come from any other place, at any other time. The junk would have been wrong. Or someone might have cared.

On January 3, 2012, the "classic lineup" of Dayton-based rock band Guided by Voices appeared on the *Late Show with David Letterman*. Guided by Voices has always represented exactly the kind of fucked-up we understand, especially in its earliest incarnation—a brilliant singer and lyricist stuck in a schoolteaching job; a guitarist who looked like an adjunct professor; another guitarist who looked as if he were in Black Flag; a bassist who looked like one of Herman's Hermits. Up until, say, the Internet, the best Ohio rock bands always looked like this: an intuitive, adamant imitation of something we thought we were getting right (but probably weren't) while also pretending we didn't care (but did).

And then, through the usual series of inexplicable circumstances, Guided by Voices became one of the most influential bands of the 1990s and 2000s, and one of the most beloved, sort of the Grateful Dead of indie rock. The singer, Robert Pollard, was the only constant through all those years, and the original members never got to experience the height of the band's success.

So then, nearly thirty years after their formation, those original members, now middle-aged, made their network television debut. You might call this a moment of nostalgia, as long as you recognize the difference between nostalgia and sentimentality. Nostalgia is what a friend of mine from Youngstown calls "happiness rusted over."

Letterman held up the new album, introduced the band, and off they went.

Guided by Voices kicked in immediately with earnest deliberation, playing a new song, "The Unsinkable Fats Domino," a terse staccato with open spaces between power chords. In the opening moments, guitarist Mitch Mitchell strummed a chord and struck a pose, hand raised in the devil-horn configuration. Fifteen seconds later, bass player Greg Demos, sporting his trademark striped bell-bottoms, made his own rock move, bobbing intensely to the beat, then spreading his legs wide, and then his feet went out from under him and down he went, hard, on his ass.

The moment was beautiful, a complete triumph of a truth well-known in Dayton and Akron and all these other places: we are the ones who always try too hard. That's how we rise and that's how we fall. And there isn't much difference between the two.

I was riding in my friend Jim's car, eighteen years old, going nowhere. He was driving with one hand and punching his other fist against the ceiling to the beat of "Precious," the first track on the first Pretenders album, two chords set against a heavy backbeat with an odd time signature that all led up to Chrissie Hynde's epic, sultry, post-guitar-lead vocal breakdown that, as far as I was concerned, was equal to any Robert Plant squeeze-my-lemon invocation and also was the first time I had ever heard a grown woman say the word *fuck*. It was thrilling.

After an unhinged squall of lead guitar, the rhythm section dropped into a driving, primal drumbeat, the bass continuing underneath, as Hynde, sounding earnestly, ambitiously jaded, riffed on about feeling *ethereal*, and having her eye on an *imperial* and something about Howard the Duck and Mr. Stress, an impressionistic scat that rose to a steel-tongued testimony: "But not me baby, I'm too precious . . . Fuck off!"

Let the mad punching begin.

So Jim rammed his fist rhythmically against the ceiling, and the other three of us all soon followed because what else are you gonna do? Four of us in a Pontiac on a late-spring afternoon with six Mickey's big mouths between us and a two-quarter-time pulse buzzing from the blown speakers, punching the ceiling as hard as we possibly could. It doesn't hurt under those conditions. Testosterone in high doses produces in the human male a temporary imperviousness not just to pain but sensitivity to every human feeling except lust (which is of course indelible). We punched away, feeling it, until, one by one, we stopped to listen to that climax:

But not me, baby, I'm too precious . . . Fuck off!

And then began punching again.

After a while, it did start to hurt. When the song ended, in the tape hiss before the next track, "The Phone Call," began, I ventured: "Why are we doing this?"

Jim turned around in the driver's seat and looked at me, wild euphoria mixing with vague disappointment and judgment. "Because this is what we *do*."

So, for the time being at least, I had no real context for this song, whose lyrics were explicitly about the place where we'd grown up, with lines about "moving to the Cleveland heat" and direct references to streets we knew—East Fifty-Fifth and Euclid Avenue and the Shoreway, so when Chrissie Hynde sang "duet duet duet do it on the pavement," I knew exactly which pavement she meant, which, for me anyway, made for a peculiar, tangibly harsh specificity in an otherwise uncertain sexual fantasy. I had seen those streets and their scattered gravel and ground glass. Doing it on that pavement would be very uncomfortable.

But I wondered most about another line.

I had the album at home on vinyl, and at first, joined by Ralph in clandestine congress, with the volume set low enough that we didn't think our parents could hear, we repeatedly moved the needle back over the previous few grooves, to hear her say it again: "not me baby, I'm too precious . . . fuck off!" The imprecision of the needle drop, however, meant that most of the time I also heard the previous phrase: "Howard the Duck and Mr. Stress both stayed, trapped in a world that they never made." I knew Howard the Duck was some sort of druggy comic-book character from Cleveland; copies of those comics were passed around high school along with Harvey Pekar's *American Splendor*, and they'd begun to replace Sgt. Rock and Batman. Howard the Duck comics were like rumors of cocaine, part of some subculture that I knew existed but only in theory. And I knew from *Scene*, the local music paper, which I picked up every Thursday at the record store up at the strip plaza, that Mr. Stress was the name of a popular Cleveland blues band.

Trapped in a world that they never made.

This song was a story about where I lived. But I couldn't put it all together, and before I ever had a chance, Chrissie Hynde spit the expletive again and I moved the needle once more. Repetition, more than anything else, is the curse of adolescence—you do everything over and over and you never feel that you've gotten it right and then something new comes along and further confounds you and you never have a chance to get back to the original conundrum.

But the most important thing was something we did know for sure: Chrissie Hynde was *from here*. That meant something. She was a rock star. She was famous. And she was from here. To us, that was proof that we were from *somewhere*. Sometimes we would drive by a house we had been told was her parents' house, where they still lived, where we imagined maybe she had lived. Which meant this woman whose voice had captivated us existed, for our purposes, in two specific places:

1. Inside the red leather jacket and matching high-heeled boots on the cover of Sire Records #6083-2 . . .

and

2. There in the rustic, contemporary bungalow on Olentangy Drive, a short distance from our own homes.

The song ended on Jim's tape deck and I stopped punching because my knuckles were hurting, but Jim kept going, looking back at us wild-eyed, and I wasn't sure if I was wrong for not wanting to join him or he was wrong for continuing. So I punched with all my might, but only against the gauze that draped from the steel, faking it.

By the time the Bank was established as the center of Akron's music scene, all of those artists—Devo and the Waitresses and Chrissie Hynde and Lux Interior and the rest—were *from* here. None of them had stayed. They'd all gone off—to London and New York and LA—and so, like the empty factories, they left the impression of something that had been profoundly here and now was profoundly gone, and so recently gone that their energy field remained. There was a mood, a tension, that lingered.

What happened amid the whole "Akron sound," "new Liverpool" hype was a feeding frenzy, with record-label talent scouts flying in from all directions, combing through the clubs and the local 45s in the record-shop bins, mining for gold. So by the time I arrived at the Bank, a highly unusual culture had been established. Almost every significant original rock band remaining in Akron had either (a) been signed to a major label and somehow failed to make it any further; (b) not gotten signed and therefore carried an unusual burden of rejection for what would otherwise be a normal state of affairs for a local band; or (c) formed with the delusion that celebrity and commercial success were not only possible, but probable.

Everyone who has ever formed a rock band believed at some level that he was going to become famous. Few ever did it in a context so psychologically complex as early-1980s Akron, Ohio, a place that had always believed it was bigger than maybe it really was.

This put me, and just about anyone else of my generation with an interest in music and art and celebrity, in an interesting position. Although all of this prime activity had begun in the traditional model of the DIY underground, and all of this had happened recently and literally within the same footsteps I traveled every day, I only knew about it through the mass media, which is to say from above and afar.

The first time I heard of Devo was when they played on *Saturday Night Live*. I found out afterward they were from my hometown. I saw the Waitresses on MTV before I ever saw them play in a club. This created a strange disconnect, and a strange relationship to the idea of associating more closely with someone famous because he or she came from the same place as we did. In theory, I should have felt no more kinship to the Pretenders than I felt to, say, Dexys Midnight Runners. But that wasn't the case. And it wasn't the case because Chrissie Hynde's parents lived around the corner from my cousin. Which is obviously meaningless, except I put a great deal of meaning into that correspondence. Somehow, in my mushy and convoluted logic, because I could identify the mailbox of the parents of a young woman who played in a rock band in London that I saw in music videos in my living room on national cable television, I wasn't nobody.

The other, and perhaps most important, aspect of this was that I was significantly aware of having Just Missed Something Important. Just a few years before, these clubs and stages had been vital and exciting. Robert Christgau, the rock critic for the *Village Voice*, had come to Akron and lived here for a week, reporting a lengthy, thorough, deeply insightful, and thrilling story about the significance and range of Akron's rock scene. Not Cleveland, even though it was the perceived cultural center of our region (sometimes called the Paris of the Rust Belt), but Akron. Because it was special. I knew this had just happened, and so I was achingly aware of its absence. I had just missed something musically, culturally, artistically important, just as I had just missed the importance of Akron industrially. What does it mean to be eighteen years old, to begin defining yourself as a particular individual, in a particular place, *of* that particular place, when that place has just lost its own identity?

It means you begin to define yourself in a void. It means you learn how to listen for echoes. It means you begin looking at empty bank buildings as opportunity.

The Generics are opening for the Wombats. The Wombats have signed with Bomp Records. This is huge. We know Bomp Records. That's the label name on the back of the Stiv Bators solo record, the one he made with the guitar player he stole from the Dead Boys, whom the Dead Boys stole from Hammer Damage. John Puglia and I talk about these things as though we know these people and their gossip. As though we have taken a side in the Hammer Damage / Dead Boys controversy. We talk about how the Wombats are leaving on tour the next day as though they had shared this information with us in the dressing room, which is rumored to be accessible via a secret trapdoor from the bank vault.

We have never actually seen the Wombats.

The Wombats take the stage. Either the one guitar player is unnaturally tall or the other guitar player is unnaturally short, or (probably) a combination of both, but juxtaposed they look like mutant versions of Bomp Record Recording Artists the Wombats, or however we had imagined them, which I suppose is something overly romanticized, like Joe Perry in a band with Link Wray. Which they are not. They look like two wrong pieces that got stuck together. The one guitar is buzzing so badly that everyone is yelling at the little guy and trying to find him a better cord. The lead microphone is not working properly, but neither is the backup mic, so the singer takes them both and clamps them together in some misguided equation of sonic math, which fails.

I have no idea this is terrible. These are the Wombats and they have a record contract and they are going on tour.

The Bank was dying. I didn't know that then. I didn't have any sense of where these things came from and where they went and how tentative they always are, these places of minor personal legend. Ball fields, dance halls, banking institutions—they are all born dying and their moment of being alive is just that—a moment.

*   *   *

Ralph and I went one final time that winter before the Bank closed. We set out in one of those Ohio snowfalls that feels as if it were wrapping you up in itself for transport to another dimension, thick and deep and utterly transforming. The snow piled high even on the overhead wires and on the sidearms of light poles and draped itself into curved scallops over the heads of the elemental brick buildings that lined Main Street downtown. We had left home late, ten o'clock or so, and the snow had stopped falling by then, so that when we parked and got out of the car to cross the street to the club, a dense silence muted the scene.

Akron was approaching the depth of its despair, close enough that its desperation felt alive, almost vibrant. This did not strike me as a paradox. It suggested possibility, adventure, a rough draft of legend. Many of the buildings downtown were abandoned. We'd heard that someone had broken into the Hony Wayne and happened into a room where a mattress was covered with blood and had done what seemed the only thing to do in a situation that was settling across all of us then: nothing. Because in a situation like that, the right thing doesn't exist.

Ralph and I went into the Bank, and it was warm inside, and yellow-gray, and we stayed and watched and listened and drank until closing. When we left and walked back outside and stepped from the sidewalk, we saw only one set of tire tracks in the snow: our own, from hours before, leading to where we'd parked the car. We followed them back home.

867-5309: A LOVE SONG

Sometimes my home did feel like the middle of nowhere. Or more accurately (and worse) like a confounding void in the middle of somewhere. Everything of note that was from here was literally *from* here. If it became known, it was almost a given that it no longer existed here. Devo, transplanted in Los Angeles, referred derisively to their Ohio hometown as "a good place to be from." Chrissie Hynde, expatriated to England, wrote her long-distance ode to Akron: "My City Was Gone." Even Firestone, one of the city's signature corporations—motto: "The name that's known is Firestone"—moved its headquarters away. And not once, but twice. First to Chicago, then back to Akron, then to Nashville, all within four years, as though to underscore and amplify its departure.

It seemed that if anything had potential, it left. It began to seem necessary, the only option. Half my high school class was gone by the end of graduation summer, and the others trickled away, one after the next after the next. And conversely, everything of interest came, conspicuously, from elsewhere. Whatever we saw on television or heard on the radio or read in a magazine came from another place, and almost always the big cultural centers—New York or Los Angeles or, occasionally, Canada. Which made us seem even more disconnected.

So it was with considerable interest, in the summer of 1982, that I heard this harmonized chorus . . . a song, a hit on the radio, by the band Tommy Tutone . . . a song of obsession, of unrequited love, for a girl named Jenny, whose number was found on a bathroom wall:

Eight six seven five three oh ni-ee-niyne . . .

Eight? Six? Seven?

I put my ear toward the radio. I heard it again, a startlingly familiar series of numbers. This was a local telephone exchange, and not just a local exchange, but the one in my own neighborhood. Everyone I knew in the blocks surrounding my house had a number that started with an 8, and most of them started with that very one—867. Somebody had written a song about where I lived, and it was a good song, and it was a hit. My slowly emerging sense of art suggested that the most important songs were about real-life experiences, which was why everyone seemed so crazy about Bruce Springsteen, because everyone who listened to him literally had a "hungry heart" and could therefore relate personally to his lyrics. But now there was a song about a real-life experience that was not a familiar generalization; it actually referred to a specific aspect of my own life experience.

America was vast and fascinating in its every region, infinite in its telephonic numerology, and the writer of that song (who was from California!) could have picked any exchange to represent any place—or could have picked 555-5309 to represent every place (which would inevitably have represented no place). But he didn't. This Jenny person could be living a block away.

We knew what we had to do. We went to the basement, where a wall-mounted telephone was next to the washer and dryer, useful for teenage privacies. My older brother took his position as overseer. I lifted the receiver and dialed: 8 . . . 6 . . . 7 . . . 5 . . . 3 . . . 0 . . . 9 . . .

"Hello?"

I didn't have a lot of experience talking on the phone to girls, and so the notion of cold-calling—and particularly someone famous—took all the nerve I could muster.

"Is? . . . Is Jenny th—"

Click.

It would be years before I learned the full truth of the song. The cowriter, Alex Call, said in 2004 that he was looking for a simple pop hook, and something about the rhythm and syntax of those numbers found their way more or less randomly through his imagination.

"Despite all the mythology to the contrary, I actually just came up with the 'Jenny,' and the telephone number and the music and all that just sitting in my backyard," he told an interviewer for songfacts.com. "There was no Jenny. I don't know where the number came from, I was just trying to write a four-chord rock song, and it just kind of came out. . . . I made it up under a plum tree in my backyard."

Under a plum tree. In California. This would suggest the meaningfulness-to-catchiness ratio was approximately that of "a-wop-bop-a-loo-mop-a-wop-bam-boom."

Bruce Springsteen would later write a song called "Youngstown," about the actual Youngstown, with a love interest also named Jenny.

Here in Youngstown,
My sweet Jenny, I'm sinkin' down . . .

The name was literal, drawn from local history, and is well-known in that beleaguered city. Jenny was the town's nickname for the Jeanette Blast Furnace, part of a vibrant steel mill that shut down in 1977. Jenny sat rusting for two decades until its demolition in 1996, a year after Springsteen's song came out.

This bold adherence to fact and emotional truth seemed almost like a make-up call from the songwriter community. But far too little and far too late for me.

It took a while for the news to reach us, mostly because it wasn't really "news" so much as the opposite of news, but somehow that summer we learned there were 867–5309s in other places—apparently lots of other places—and the one that was getting all the attention was the home phone number of the daughter of the Buffalo chief of police, who was pretty unhappy about the whole thing.

Which meant we were nobody again.

We kept calling the local number from time to time because more than anything else, that's what teenage boys do: the same thing over and over, expecting different results. But we never so much as got the satisfaction of being yelled at, and soon we learned that even that part of the unraveling myth was not exclusively ours; apparently everyone in the area code who owned a radio had thought of the same prank, and before long the seven precious numbers resulted in three atonal beeps followed by the sad, familiar refrain:

We're sorry. You have reached a number that has been disconnected or is no longer in service. If you feel you have reached this recording in error, please check the number and try your call again.

PART THREE

LOCAL MEN

AS WE GO UP, WE GO DOWN.
-GUIDED BY VOICES

THE TAJ MAHAL

The old man's bar was called the Taj Mahal because one of the ancient brothers who owned the place was something of a world traveler and had decorated the interior with photographs of himself in European capitals and on African safari and shaking hands with Pygmies and whatnot. He'd spent his life visiting ruins, which was good training for operating a tavern in downtown Akron, Ohio, as the eighties drained down. Off to one end of the bar, displayed on a table, was a large model of the actual Taj Mahal, complete with a moat that was stocked with goldfish. This was unfortunate for many reasons, but mainly because the Taj Mahal was directly across the street from the Mayflower Hotel, which had once offered the finest lodgings in town, but now was a subsidized flophouse for drunks and crazies. You don't really want goldfish swimming in open waters surrounded by people carrying glasses of alcohol, especially when you know that some of them will get the shakes before the night is through.

This was the bar where we chose to celebrate John Puglia's "bachelor party," such as it was. No strippers, no tequila shots, no wild night in Vegas with a bunch of friends. John was getting married in a week, and the two of us wanted to go somewhere authentic, which notion was important to us—him studying art and me studying creative writing—even if we would never say such a thing publicly. Authenticity is something all young men crave, which is why we sometimes wear fedoras and restore cranky British motorcycles and listen to Frank Sinatra and why suspenders occasionally come back into fashion.

We'd grown up in a no-man's-land between two eras: the first, one of microdefined parochialism, and the second, one of amorphous mass culture. John and I were part of the first generation that didn't directly associate all of our defining local institutions with a corresponding local founding figure. The daily newspaper, the *Akron Beacon Journal*, founded by Charles L. Knight and groomed through the twentieth century by his son John S. Knight, had become the cornerstone of the powerful Knight Ridder newspaper chain. But while his surname was also part of a national brand, Knight, the larger-than-life man who also walked among us, had died in 1981. The major American tire companies—Goodyear, Firestone, B. F. Goodrich, and General—each had its world headquarters here, and each had scores of former workers who remembered shaking hands with the founders and figureheads. My dad always loved to tell the story about having a drink with Jerry O'Neil, the CEO and son of the founder of General Tire. But those men were gone, and while their names were on street signs and school buildings and hospitals, we had no direct connection to the humans who'd borne them.

Instead, we'd grown up with a strong sense of branding as massive, yet impersonal. Pepsi, for instance, was everywhere, and it was the same everywhere, but there was no sense of its personal mythology, its creator, its connection to any human endeavor other than consumption. It was no mistake that John had named his rock band the Generics. The arrival of generic products in our grocery stores had been a defining moment in our childhoods. Our dads proudly drank beer from a white can with black lettering that said BEER.

And this homogeneity carried all the way across the culture. National chain stores and restaurants were proliferating, with an ever-growing sense of sameness, such that one could enter a Cracker Barrel or a Waldenbooks in any city in the country and feel immediately oriented, with everything where it was supposed to be, looking the way it was supposed to look. The idea of exploration and discovery was being replaced with comfort and familiarity. It was becoming impossible to get lost, which is where the imagination thrives. Yet, even though we always knew where we were, we had a nagging sense of disorientation. If the Waldenbooks self-help aisle in Denver was identical to the one in Milwaukee and identical to the one in Jacksonville, then the idea of being *somewhere* was more like being *anywhere*, which is uncomfortably close to the idea of being *nowhere*, or of *where* being an irrelevant notion altogether.

So John and I weren't directly defined by our place, not the way our parents had been. And we couldn't be defined by what was replacing it because that was impossible. We were watching all of the old institutions that had given our city its personality be replaced by boxes containing TGI Friday's and Super K-Mart—things that defined everybody's life the same way, which means they didn't define anyone's in any particular way.

Gold Circle had gone under, and although it was a chain, it was regional; it was close to home, and so it had some connection to my sense of place. I liked when I went to another state and realized they didn't have a Gold Circle there, that it was somehow more mine because it wasn't theirs. Other places had their own version of this—Piggly Wiggly or Big Bear. In a similar spirit, I was particularly fond of obscure rock bands because, when I found someone else who was a fan of, say, Hüsker Dü or Bush Tetras, it created a bond. (Unfortunately, this sometimes devolved into the inevitable affliction of choosing obscure things solely for the sake of their obscurity, the effect of which was a record collection with a considerable percentage of terrible music. But still.)

So John and I had taken to exploring our downtown, a place almost nobody went, with some sense of purpose and even maybe urgency. Main Street seemed increasingly intimate because it belonged to increasingly fewer people and increasingly fewer people belonged to it. The act of consciously choosing it as ours seemed like a membership.

Then again, an inventory of the Taj Mahal's clientele suggested that maybe this was not such a hard (or desirable) association to crack. Many of the patrons were entirely defined by their deficiencies, in the way the characters of a formula detective novel are defined by their singular traits, and not just defined, but named: Toothless, One-Leg, Lumpy. They wore their drunkenness like hundred-pound cloaks. It covered them completely and bent them down. Half of them were socially withdrawn in ways that made newcomers uncomfortable; the other half were socially outgoing to the same effect.

Again, this was where we went to celebrate John's last night as a bachelor.

The man started a conversation with John. His name was Bob. He spoke in an affectedly elegant voice, the kind that takes dictation from a thesaurus. In the way that Hollywood used to attach an English accent to anyone sophisticated, regardless of nationality (Ashley Wilkes, Nazi officers, Roman senators, etc.), Bob seemed to have taken the continental route to his barstool at the Taj Mahal.

"What do you know of beauty?" he asked, first looking at John, then at me.

I didn't know how to answer the question, and John didn't either, but he was quicker on his feet and better at these games.

"What do *you* know of beauty?" John responded with a sideways laugh, turning the question back to the old man. John was always best as a catalyst.

Sitting next to Bob was a friend of his, a short, sturdy man with thick gray hair, neatly combed, and an elaborately waxed mustache. His name was Jerry and we knew him mainly for his public presence trolling the sidewalks wearing a sandwich board for one of the few downtown restaurants, which he did in return for being allowed to display his paintings there. He wore a suit with wide lapels, no tie, the collar of his shirt overlapping his jacket. Everything was just *so*. He smelled strongly of soap, which for some reason never makes a person smell clean.

He lived in the Mayflower. He said he had a studio there, and the way he said the word *studio* suggested he took the work he did there seriously, with a little extra emphasis on the *u* syllable.

"I have one piece that I painted," he told me. "It's a boy, and a dog. Both of them are on the grass, with their bellies down on the ground, staring, face-to-face. They're tugging on a piece of rope. The boy's holding it in his hand; the dog has it in his teeth. And they're facing off. It is not a sentimental piece. It is realism. I call it *Best Friend*. The title is ambiguous. Is the boy the dog's best friend? "Or"—brief dramatic pause—"is the dog the boy's best friend?"

The Jerry I knew in the daytime—the downtown I knew in the daytime—held for me the same allure as, say, the music of Tom Waits and the notion of firing a Winchester: an exotic mystique that seemed directly American, slightly distant and illuminated, something directly of who and what I was, but also something "other," something John and I both wanted to understand. Jerry in the nighttime, however, was a bit close for comfort, and I suppose by extension implied that maybe Tom Waits was just an excellent trickster and that I'd look foolish absorbing the kick of an anachronistic firearm. I didn't know how to maintain my end of this conversation and drifted back toward John's.

Bob was still talking about beauty, becoming more specific, talking about a woman's beauty and then a woman's flesh and then a woman's pink flesh. When he took a drink, he held it in his mouth for a while, not so much as if he were savoring, but as though in some brief indecision about swallowing it, although the only other option would be to spit it out, and I seriously doubt anyone in the Taj Mahal ever spit liquor out on purpose.

"These people here, these are poor people," he said. "Not poor in money. I don't mean that. But poor in beauty. They have not been given the opportunities that we have had to see the beauty of the world. So they are poor. But it's not their fault."

I wondered what it meant to put on a suit to go to a bar like this, not a business suit or a funeral suit, but what Bob might call a "suit of clothes," something to complete a man. Bob came across as the fading shadow of an *Esquire* man, of the Norman Mailer *Esquire*. His Wild Turkey was Glenlivet; his polyester was vicuña. I was wearing an untucked oxford shirt, which simultaneously made me feel conspicuously overdressed, like a college boy misplaced in an old man's bar (which I was), and also, in the shadow of Bob, underdressed. Either way, I didn't fit.

But John did. Because John knew how to listen and he knew how to banter. He worked part-time in a rubber factory. This was a good way to understand how to talk to people because the conversation on the shop floors never stopped. Not ever. That was how those guys got through eight hours of dirty, monotonous work: by talking over (or against, really) the machinery. I was listening to Jerry, but I think I was just a convenient replacement for his usual audience of half-conscious drunkards. John, however, was having an actual conversation with Bob. They were getting somewhere.

"Do you know what snooker is?"

John and I looked at Bob. I thought it might be some kind of profane euphemism, but I wasn't sure.

"No," we both said.

Snooker is a game like pool, Bob told us, but stressed that it was a "gentleman's game." He mentioned Sir Neville Chamberlain and again the notion of gentlemanliness, noting that we, all of us in this group, were gentlemen, and that we should play snooker.

The accuracy of this notion of the four of us as "gentlemen" aside, the Taj Mahal didn't have a pool table. Before anyone had a chance to make this observation, Bob had risen from his chair, slid a few bills onto the bar, smoothed the front of his blazer, and turned toward the door, pausing to indicate we should follow.

I looked at John. He looked at me. I knew he wanted to go along. I wanted to want to go along too, but something was beginning not to feel right. The more Bob and Jerry drank, the more red and watery their eyes became, and the more slurry their speech. Whatever distinction they made between themselves and the rest of the Mayflower/Taj Mahal community seemed to be eroding. Jerry had continued to regale me with stories of his life in art, and to make random references to the likes of Degas and Miró and Monet, whom he called a hack. He talked a lot about technique, about using charcoals to capture the darkness of the human condition and so forth, but it was all beginning to sound like things he'd heard or read somewhere, and not like something he understood from his own experience.

Nevertheless, we all got up, paid, and headed toward the door, following Bob.

"To the Met Lounge," he said.

The Met Lounge was almost directly across Main Street, another low-rent tavern that was a holdover from what people were beginning to call the "old days," which actually had not been long before, when the Akron day was regulated by three factory-shift changes, which, in turn, represented three drinking shifts. As the prevailing culture had disintegrated, the falling of its pieces into new hands was clunky and random. Some places, such as the

Bank, had been readapted in a low-rent sort of way before being abandoned again. Others were still running down the last revolutions of their decline, and this described the Met, which was basically the Taj Mahal without the charm or the moat but with a pool table. A story about the Met made the rounds, about how two frat boys happened in one night to find the place empty except for the barmaid, who'd fallen asleep sitting on her stool, chin propped against the heel of her hand. They decided to steal the Ms. Pac-Man machine. They unplugged it and began to carry it out the back door, but got stuck halfway through, and the struggle to get it free woke the barmaid and foiled the plot.

The four of us got ourselves situated at the pool table with fresh drinks, and Bob began to enlighten us on the game of snooker, which didn't sound any different to me from pool. I couldn't quite follow his instructions, so when we began, I just tried to hit the balls toward the pockets, and since I was a terrible pool player, I missed right away and nobody knew if I understood the rules or not.

This went on for a while, but as it did, Bob began to lose what remained of his elegance; his eyes reddened and he started to call John "my boy," and by about the third use of the phrase it sounded like a cruelty and then he had John in a headlock.

I had never been in a bar fight and I definitely did not want to start this way, with a drunk, old man, but John's face was deeply flushed and alarm was in his eyes, his head twisted sideways, hair askew. Bob appeared to be applying as much force as he could, and John arched his back and twisted his shoulders, trying to break free. Jerry had taken a seat at the bar and seemed not to recognize what was happening, and I was wishing I could do the same.

What was the protocol here? Can you punch someone old enough to be your grandfather? Can you bark out a command to him? Is he the responsibility of his friend? Do you ask the bartender for advice?

John, I think, had been working through the same moral dilemma, albeit to a more urgent degree. He was younger and stronger, but it took what seemed an eternity—in reality, maybe half a minute—for physical instinct to take over. Finally, his face now deep red, he grabbed Bob's forearm with both hands and pried the choke hold loose, yanking his head free and holding Bob at arm's length while he ran the fingers of his other hand against his neck.

"*Je*-sus," he said, half-trying to laugh but mostly incredulous.

"That's how you play snooker," Bob said, his diction all raw and broken free of its aristocratic restraint. "My boy."

John and I quickly downed our drinks and left.

John S. Knight's newspaper the *Akron Beacon Journal* was housed in a stately art deco building, solid and imposing. It had that steadying effect that good institutions have. But most people didn't acknowledge the building for its lower architecture. They knew it for the giant, gaudy, rotating digital clock mounted on its top, one of the most prominent features of the downtown landscape.

The building dated to 1930, and the clock was added in the 1960s. This gangly, rotating rectangular spire, twenty-six feet tall, was turquoise, with the time and temperature flashing on two opposing panels and the huge, illuminated red plastic initials of the newspaper on the other two panels. So the local newspaper's defining symbol was a giant shaft thrusting into the sky, advertising BJ all night in bright red lights.

John and I called this "our" clock. This is how downtown was then. It was all personal. Your timepiece was a gleaming tower five stories above the street. You owned empty hotels and banks and canals and city streets. They were exclusively ours because they had lost their exclusivity. In many ways, within the central city, we felt like the luckiest generation ever to have lived here. Everything was left to us and was ours to reinvent. When we left the Met Lounge, the BJ clock told us it was still early. We would have enough time to go over to the factory.

Downtown's main street, which with very industrial and Midwestern purpose was called Main Street, covered exactly one mile through the business district, which was by then characterized by grimy windows blanked out by yellowing newspapers, taped there by forlorn landlords. Storefronts were littered with the remnants of the last claims whose stakes had been removed. A mannequin's arm. A lady's hat. Discontinued greeting cards. The city, desperate to attract tenants, had attempted an incentive campaign with a Monopoly theme, so now these windows also included faded, water-stained posters mimicking a game board, with a monocled cartoon aristocrat imploring anyone who might pass by to pick up property cheap. Land on Main Street. Collect $200.

This stretch of the central city made an Oz-like transition into the vast, sprawling, mostly abandoned campus of the B. F. Goodrich company, a science-fiction backlot, and that's where John and I were headed, lit by the glow of our clock and the random greasy-yellow lights of cockeyed upstairs windows.

Goodrich was the first tire company in Akron, the one that had set into motion the uncanny growth of the industry and the city, from a canal town that produced clay products—sewer pipes and marbles and teacups and glazed figurines—to a place that was entirely defined by things made of rubber. Akron became known as the Rubber City and had a Wonka-like fantasy to it all, as latex was poured into great vats, mixed with powdered carbon black, and came out as tires and belts and hoses and shoe soles and rafts and balloons and baby dolls and blimps. In the heyday, a street in Akron was paved with rubber, and people here, growing more confident in their own possibility, believed this would further prove the absolute worthiness of the city and its product:

Soon every town in America would pave its roads with rubber!

Unfortunately, the experiment fizzled. When the rubber road was examined after a decade of use, engineers determined that the surface fared about as well as regular asphalt, which cost three times less than the rubber paving material.

Akron, meanwhile, became defined by dense neighborhoods extending from the factories, populated by people who branded themselves variously as "Goodyear families" or "Firestone families" or "Goodrich families" or "Mohawk families," and so on.

But nowhere was the cityscape more fantastical than in the acres and acres of the Goodrich complex. As the company grew, Goodrich developed a renaissance flair, taking on contracts that expanded its personality by tangents and exponents. The company would get a contract to make shoes and would build a little brick factory on the grounds specifically for shoes. There was a facility for rubber bands, another for golf balls, one for automotive hoses, and so on. In the 1960s, Goodrich landed a government contract to make space suits and hired local seamstresses to sew the space-age fabric into uniforms for Project Mercury astronauts, turning them into otherworldly Rosie the Riveters. In Akron, they made the suit John Glenn was wearing when he became the first American to orbit the earth. So the campus grew into a dense, haphazard maze of forty-five brick buildings in all sizes and shapes, from the hulking, six-story tire factory at its leading edge to single-room shops tucked here and there, to an ornate headquarters with a fanciful clock set into a bridge between two office towers. The industrial village was intercut with streets and alleys, crisscrossed with pedestrian bridges and walkways, and—maybe, or so John and I had heard—connected underground by a complex network of mysterious tunnels.

Now it was dark and empty. The headquarters had moved out toward the suburbs, and only a fraction of the local workforce remained—about fourteen hundred people, most of whom would be laid off within the next couple of years. Goodrich had begun something it called Operation Greengrass—a plan to raze the entire complex and plant grass seed. Soon it would be gone.

We slipped around a brick corner into the black shadows and found a barrel to boost us up to a ladder and then we began to climb. It didn't take long to find an opening to one of the main factory buildings. We each swung our legs over a sill and stepped down onto a concrete floor, glass and debris crunching under our feet. There was a complex sound of fluttering and scurrying, and the dripping of sourceless water.

It was less dark inside than I'd expected with the accumulated light of all those windows, half of them broken, the other half grimy, a kind of dingy glow, mostly from the moon.

"Jesus," John said. "It's big."

We'd both poked around down here, a lot, but I had never been inside one of the main buildings, and even in the dark its solidity and scale was impressive. Despite the decay, the overwhelming sense was of how well built this place was, of its enduring, defining quality.

No machines were left. Akron was filled with men haunted by a particular lament, a story told again and again: the same hands that had worked a machine for years had had to unbolt that machine, dismantle it, and crate it up to be shipped overseas where a cheaper worker would use it. These men were desperate to remake their lives. Through the 1980s, they scraped for any kind of work. Many had simply disappeared, gone South or West or just plain down into their basements. They were telling their children to get out as soon as they were able.

But much of what John and I loved about Akron was the very argument those fathers were making: the abandoned landscape, the hard challenge, the long odds. We saw the same things but in a very different way, with an absolute belief that something was to be saved here, that lives were to be made, that we could remake all this as our own.

This was the central question of our place, of all places like this, of the entire industrial Midwest, the Rust Belt, a question teetering on this very moment:

Is it something beyond salvation, or something to be saved? And what exactly is "it"?

Not long before, a columnist from the *Beacon Journal* had gone down Main Street, counting empty storefronts. In that stretch of a mile, he found fifty-two of them, businesses that had gone under. John and I calculated that as fifty-two places we could get cheap. We would start a magazine, make documentaries, build a sculpture garden.

It was all possibility.

Concrete pillars, fluted at each end, stretched from floor to ceiling, covered with graffiti: jagged letters and swirls of paint and tagger signatures layered one over the next. It was hard to make out the details, but some of it was elaborate. Murals covered some of the walls.

John followed the lure of one of these paintings, walking into the shadows for a closer look. It was creepy enough in there that I wanted to stay close and I moved to catch up with him. And that's when I saw it, all at once, opening in the dark like a phantom.

"John!" I screamed. "Stop!"

He froze and turned back to look at me. "What?"

"Stop!"

"What?"

"Look in front of you."

There, one step ahead: an open elevator shaft.

We continued, much more carefully, making our way up stairwells, lost in the exploration. In the dark, we found hints of people's lives. A glove, a stack of work orders. Someone had written a message on a door:

ALL GONE
NO WORK

We found a staircase and made our way up, one turn, then the next and the next until we found a door that opened to the roof and then there we were, high up in the air, stepping out to the sky. We strode across the rubber roof as though it were a small frontier and leaned our elbows atop the parapet to see the glittering lights of the city that had all grown from here, this very spot. More than a hundred years before, the entire identity, the entire future, the entire legacy, of our city had begun on this very corner, when Benjamin Franklin Goodrich, an entrepreneurial New Yorker, had chosen Akron over all his other options.

We looked out into the night. The air was cool. The lights stretched farther than I expected. Forever, in every direction.

THE POET'S ASSISTANT

I suppose when you finish an English degree and turn to the local newspaper help-wanted ads looking for literary work, you deserve what you get. The classifieds had two listings under "Writing." One was for a professional résumé service that was called, conveniently, A Professional Résumé Service, the *A* appended to the company name in the manner of exterminators and locksmiths vying for top billing in the yellow pages. The other was for a poet in need of an assistant. Where I come from, that sort of job opportunity does not often appear in the classifieds. This was like finding a listing for "sorcerer's apprentice" or "journeyman self-pleasurer." I called.

The woman on the phone had a name that sounded like a pen name, curly and alliterative, delivered with an accent that was exotic and full of tongue, evoking desert sand and mosques and figs. She lived in a condominium development that I knew was filled with rich people, and she asked me to come by in the evening. I drove there in my secondhand 1980 Chevrolet Citation, a car that had aged so profoundly it looked as though it had wasting disease. It was not even eight years old, but had already been through a clutch, two starters, and a chronic series of brake problems. Discolored blotches had developed in the blue paint of the hood. I'd repaired the broken plastic turn-signal/headlight assembly with sheet-metal screws and Super Glue so it looked like Frankenstein's bad eye. The windshield leaked badly, and the rain-water that settled under the driver's seat had caused the floor and seat brackets to rust out. I repaired it with scrap lumber, so my car was slowly beginning to resemble a hay wagon. If you own a crap car long enough, eventually the entire thing becomes homemade.

I arrived at the address and parked the Citation (a car that I'd come to realize was named for a traffic ticket) at the curb, hoping it would look less unflattering from a distance in the dusk. I had brought a copy of my résumé, which I'd padded enough to fill two-thirds of a page, including my ball-boy experience, but mostly listing surveying and landscaping and construction jobs and a stint on a loading dock—jobs I'd loved because they were the sorts of jobs that felt authentic, but at the same time looked entirely unsatisfying on a printed page. I also included the titles of a couple of short stories published in the university's literary journal and a short essay I'd entered in the local newspaper's holiday writing contest, which was awarded the same "honorable mention" shared by all the other also-rans. Pretty much, then, I had nothing.

I touched the glowing button next to the front door and heard chimes echo from the other side. She opened the door, a late-middle-aged woman, well fed, black hair streaked with gray, dressed in a shapeless, layered, silky, multicolored robelike dress that covered her like a set of draperies. She stood there a moment without saying anything, nodded her head, and said, "You look great."

First of all, women never told me I looked "great." The best I ever got was "cute." Mostly I got "nonthreatening." What I looked was perpetually ten years younger than my real age. I'd put on a pair of khakis that felt entirely like someone else's pants, which they were because I'd borrowed them from my brother, and I'd buttoned the top button at the collar of my white, thrift-store dress shirt because that look seemed to work for Peter Gabriel and David Byrne, both of whom were gainfully employed. My hair, which I preferred to rub around in a circle until it turned into sort of a bird's nest, was matted down and touched with gel.

I wore big, black-framed glasses that had, on the loading dock, earned me the nickname Elvis Costello, which is not a good nickname to have on a loading dock, and a pair of loafers that looked as if I'd pulled them off a sleeping drunk. Men are almost always willing to believe a woman who pays them a physical compliment and in fact will use it as a launching pad for an exaggeration of what was actually said, but standing there at the doorstep of a mysterious poet who was advertised to be in need of an assistant, I could not avoid the obvious. I did not look great and this woman had a reason other than objectivity for saying I did.

She invited me in. The condominium was lushly decorated, all with the same accent of her diction, something deep and balmy and herby whose origin eluded me entirely, mostly because I'd never been anywhere more exotic than the Canadian side of Niagara Falls.

We entered the living room and she gestured for me to sit. The chair was deep and plush and I felt as if I wouldn't be able to spring from it quickly if I had to, which (for some reason was something) I was thinking might happen soon.

"Would you like a glass of wine?" she said, already pouring.

"No, thank you," I said, as she turned and handed it toward me.

I accepted it and set it on the table beside me. She sat on a couch across from me, crossing her legs at an angle, draping an arm across the couch's back.

"So," she said, nodding, and narrowing her eyes, examining me for a long moment before continuing, "Have you heard of me?"

I wasn't sure how to answer, wasn't sure why I would have heard of her, and I didn't like the question because I was sure that no was the wrong answer, but if I lied and said yes, I'd never get away with it, so I responded as carefully as I could.

"No, I'm sorry, I don't think I have."

She told me that she was under contract with a Large Commercial Publisher and that her books were doing very well and that she'd been written about in the local newspaper, although the newspaper she mentioned was not the *Beacon Journal* but rather a small weekly shopper that mostly carried verbatim press releases and photographs of ribbon cuttings and handshake ceremonies of the presentation of oversize checks. I knew enough about poetry to know that books filled with it were published mostly by small presses run by other poets, whom I imagined as middle-aged idealists with strawlike hair and overtaxed oxfords, who grew their own produce and believed deeply in Ralph Nader. These books weren't even called books. They were called chapbooks, which made them sound homespun, like something hand-lettered by lamplight at the Ingalls family table, protected by a sheet of horn. They were not generally released by large commercial publishers, and not generally referred to as "doing well." But I could have been wrong about this and was in no position to challenge.

"First," she said, "would you read for me?"

I didn't understand this question either, but before I had a chance to try, she reached over to the table beside the sofa and produced a copy of the university's literary magazine, the sight of which made me blush hotly and tighten at the sphincter and wonder how in the hell she knew about this.

I had three poems in that issue. That was bad enough. Worse was that their publication was laden with complications of ethics and legitimacy. While serving on the journal's editorial committee, I had written these poems more or less spontaneously one afternoon in the library when I was supposed to be studying. I thought the poems weren't bad, but I wasn't sure because my problem with poetry had always been an inability to distinguish the bad from the good. I loved William Carlos Williams's poem, "This Is Just to Say," which sounded like a note to his family about being sorry for eating the plums that were in the icebox but they were delicious. But then someone told me it actually *was* a note to his family about being sorry for eating delicious plums. So what until then was one of my favorite poems I now believed wasn't really a poem. Mostly I consumed poetry the way I consumed wine: I liked it all well enough and gladly partook whenever the opportunity arose, but I couldn't tell the high-end stuff from the low-end stuff, and the quantifiers of quality (metrical complexity, pathos, typicity, appellation) left me nodding my head as though I understood.

Because I couldn't properly serve on a committee that would be judging my own work, I had submitted these poems under a pseudonym, then sat nervously as the stacks of photocopied student literature were distributed among the three editors. Soon, my two colleagues, who didn't appear to have any better grasp of poetry than I did, were dispensing the sort of praise on my verse that student editors serve up like cafeteria scoops of mashed potatoes ("I really like the imagery"; "There's a relatableness there"; etc.). My ego couldn't stand the idea of not receiving these compliments directly, so I sheepishly admitted the poems were mine.

The woman reached across the void between us, handing the magazine, which she'd already folded open, to me. I accepted it like a subpoena. She half-reclined, leaning her head back, letting her eyelids relax.

"Read the first one," she said.

I had avoided looking at these words on the page ever since they had found their way there by way of the conference room where three of us somehow decided they should be in the issue but only under my real name and at the expense of my resignation from the editorial board. (Poetry is complicated, but not always in the way you think.) I had never been comfortable reading aloud to begin with, much less reading my own writing, and certainly not reading writing that included ingredients of controversy and shame.

She waited. I realized I had no choice. I began:

Hey, Snakeleg.
Why not we sublimate
The deaf girls
And teach them to dance . . .

I could feel the air draining from my voice. After a long spell of trying, I suddenly was unable to fool myself about these poems. They were really, really bad. And bad poetry is something much worse than bad hair or bad shoes or even a bad stomach. Allowing the world to see your bad poetry is a deliberate act, and all its negative consequences are deserved. Because nobody asked to see it in the first place.

We oughta
Reel in some herringbone
And watchfob his kneecaps
With brickbats and a tommydog . . .

I wanted her to tell me to stop. It would have been worth the humiliation for her to just say this is horrible and I can't listen to another word, just so I could stop hearing it myself. But she just sat there, bobbing her head.

What the hell is a tommydog? I wondered silently. *And how do you "watchfob a kneecap"?*

I finished the last line. She took a sip of her wine, reached across to the same table, and produced a hardcover book. Without introduction, she opened and began reading. I assumed this was one of her own poems and soon made out her name on the cover and listened, trying to determine if it was any good, but I'd lost any power of discernment. She finished and set the book aside.

"Well," she said, "now we know something about one another."

Not really, I thought. *Pretty much the opposite.*

She began to tell me about her family and walked me through the condo, showing me around. I was waiting for her to begin to interview me, or to tell me about the job, or even just to mention it, but the longer this went on, the more I began to doubt a job existed. She showed me a framed picture of her son, who looked to be about my age, a black-haired man in green military fatigues. He was pointing an automatic rifle at the camera.

"Very . . . nice?" I said.

I was ready to leave.

"So," she finally said, "do you want to come work for me?"

"And do what?"

"Editing and filing. Help with the mailing."

I was no poet, but I couldn't figure out any possible way this sort of work would require hiring an assistant.

"How many hours a week?"

"Oh, we'll figure that out as we go along."

"And can I ask what it pays?"

She offered less than I'd made in my last job, as a construction grunt. I said I didn't think I could get by on that. She said she thought I'd change my mind once I had a chance to think it over. I eased my way toward an exit and left a quiet, uneasy exhale as I returned down the front walk to my car. I could feel her watching me. I settled into the front seat, the wood frame creaking beneath me, and felt the same tightness return to my throat that I'd felt when she asked me to read.

The next day I called A Professional Résumé Service. I got the job and spent the next few months writing prefab cover letters for people as desperate as I was.

APARTMENT X

I was hanging upside down from the fire escape when the police arrived. Loose change fell out of my pocket, ting-tinging against the pavement. I squeezed the metal stair tighter, attempting invisibility.

Look, if you put four young men in an alley full of fire escapes under cover of darkness, one of them is going to start climbing. That's just basic math.

And this moonlit back corridor had offered a stunning array of choices. So while climbing up here seemed like the most natural and logical thing to be doing at three in the morning, the arrival of local law enforcement was cause for reconsideration.

The building to whose back I clung was the Hotel Anthony Wayne. The hotel and the adjoining Bank nightclub had been abandoned for nearly a decade, which had only enhanced their mystique.

My brother and I had spontaneously begun. I gave him a boost to the first landing of the fire escape. He reached down with one hand and pulled me up far enough that I could grasp its steel lip with my fingers and pull myself up. We couldn't get through the cage that enclosed the landing, so we started to climb the stairs on their back side, working hand over hand as though scaling a diagonal set of monkey bars from underneath. The climb was awkward; we were leaning backward, looking up toward the sky. But it wasn't hard, especially with the fuel of adventure, of discovery, and of an evening's beer.

John and our friend Larry stood at the bottom, watching, calling out instructions.

"If you go up one more set, you can get to the next landing. It's open there," John said in a stage whisper.

I watched Ralph as he led the way. He'd always been more athletic than me, and more willing to take on physical challenges. We progressed carefully—ten feet, fifteen, rising above the alley that ran behind the row of buildings, parallel to the old canal.

Every American Industrial Age city is defined by its water. For Akron, it was the canal. The city began as a rest stop on the Ohio and Erie Canal, and its entire shape and personality emerged from there. Akron was defined first by the vitality of the canal, then by its demise, and now by its charming obsolescence.

The canal smells sometimes, sewer overrun, a stench that seems to overtly demand attention. The waterway still crawls through the city, a slow, man-made riverish thing that defied geography and gravity and modernity, concrete-walled, polluted, utilitarian, unkillable. Until 1913, the canal was a main commercial vein from whose prime line the entire city was drawn. But that all ended in March of that year. The freeze-thaw-freeze cycle that defines an Ohio winter had encased the state in ice amid an Easter weekend whose meteorology seems bizarre unless you've lived here, in which case you understand why we talk so much about the weather:

Good Friday: sixty degrees and heavy rain.
Holy Saturday: twenty degrees and a hard freeze and more rain.
Easter Sunday: Heavy rain.

The frozen and saturated ground couldn't absorb the precipitation that kept on falling—nearly ten inches in total—and the entire state endured devastating flooding that killed more than 450 people and washed out more than forty thousand homes. In Akron, the rising water threatened to overwhelm all of downtown, and city officials took the drastic and permanent measure of dynamiting the canal locks north of the central city to relieve the pent-up water. With railroads already well established, that one exploding night ended the practical use of the canal. So now, like almost everything else, it remained as impressive in its form as it was adrift from its function, another remnant of a world we never made.

Abandoned, it belonged to us. An entire canal, there for the taking, along with hotels and banks and whatever else was left for dead. We were like a garage band that had found ELO's gear tossed on the curb.

In the moonlight, the shallow water was still and flat, barely moving forward, easing the bottom weeds in a slow, psychedelic dance. Whenever it rained, the canal's pace quickened, but so did that smell, as sewage found its way into the mix. This night, it lolled sleepily.

There was little direct access to the canal, just worn footpaths where the underbrush offered least resistance, but from time to time I found myself down there, rarely as a destination, most often as a matter of having escaped from the street, but always, upon arrival, wondering about this concrete stream, a shabby living history with no one to explain it. One night in high school, my friend Dave and I camped out in front of the old downtown Akron Civic Theater, first in line to buy tickets to see the Clash play there on what would become their final tour. Once we'd established our spot with sleeping bags and lawn chairs, we took occasional breaks to sneak behind the theater and shotgun contraband beers. The theater spanned the canal by way of a bridge from the main building to the back dressing rooms, and we sat underneath, listening to the soft rush of a little waterfall echoing off the pillars and the theater above us. Across the shimmering water, we could see the date 1906 stamped into the concrete wall. We tossed our cans into the water and reestablished ourselves in our position of dominance out by the ornate box office.

For several years, I was in a band that played in a shabby club called the Daily Double, a converted warehouse that overlooked the canal half a mile to the south, the slow, anachronistic stream offering a place to wander to after the gear was loaded and it felt too early to go home.

This night, then, carried the slant echo of discovery as we trooped along in the weeds. From the fire escape, the vantage of my downtown was revelatory in its way, fifty feet off the promenade, scanning the buildings from behind and slightly below. Their fronts all displayed failure, plywood and cardboard and newspaper on either side of the doorways, covering the storefronts' faces like sets of ashamed hands. Their façades were untended, cracked marble and glass, fading paint, dead neon, defeated brokers' signs, abandoned pleas. But here in the alley, the backs of the buildings seemed self-assured, the brick arches of their windows like the brows of watchful eyes, the rusty iron staircases still offering escape. Holes were punched in the brick and missing windows, but that only seemed to underscore the prevailing survival instinct, which, more than anything else, defined this heady corridor. Weeds back here were mature, a horticulture of untended urbanity rustling in the night. The oxygen they breathed out was just as good as that from orchids and hibiscus. Unperfumed, but perfectly useful. The ground was uneven brick splotched with macadam and bituminous fill. Glass crunched underfoot. Stray clumps of paper, wet and dried and wet and dried, clung to rocks and weeds like plaster of a badly formed cast.

These were some of my favorite places in the world. These buildings never seemed dead to me. I found the empty, boarded-up downtown hotels far less dead than the falsely sterile, monotonous chains that stood submissive and unadorned at every highway exit. There were no surprises there, and the antiseptic air always felt like the whisper of a lie it thought I wanted to hear. Here, the decay was honest and full of life, vibrant in its constant self-creation. Every view was a thrill. In daylight, I'd seen where small plants had taken root in the mortar of the old brick buildings, growing sideways and upward out of the wall, as though to prove defiantly there was still life to give. These buildings were constructed to last forever; despite everything that had happened in the past decade or two, they maintained that presence. The new strip malls, on the other hand, offered a cynical implication that the buildings would exist only as long as their leases, that they had no need to be beautiful or permanent, because with their green lumber and hollow blocks they could easily be demolished and replaced with a new structure that better suited the corporate footprint of the new tenant. From Shoe Carnival to Hobby Lobby in three easy steps. (Liquidate, eradicate, fabricate.)

John was separated from his wife and living in a loft space downtown that had been empty since the 1970s. The building was just across the street from the Goodrich factory where a few years before we had commemorated the beginning of his marriage. So the location had something of a bittersweetness. Despite the seeming quaintness of the term, the notion of a "downtown loft" had nothing to do with yuppie gentrification. There was no trend, no glamour, no promise of future return on an investment. As far as we knew, only one other person lived downtown as a matter of choice, a photographer who had purchased cheap space for a studio above an abandoned storefront and had turned part of his loft into his home. His space, he claimed, had once been a brothel, and he described himself sometimes as the resident whore. The rest of the downtown dwellers were in the Mayflower Hotel or, worse, invisible in doorways and stairwells, their silhouettes impressed upon piles of wear-softened cardboard and cloth.

John's apartment, decades before, had been occupied by the owner of the jewelry store two floors down. The name of the store owner—Fred A. Grimm—was memorialized in the mosaic tile at the threshold, though, like almost everything else downtown, that sign existed as a reference divorced from its referent, a puzzle piece without its mate, prompting John to make references to "Ole Lady Grimm"—a sort of specter to ease the loneliness. Now the space was occupied by a little restaurant called the Diamond Deli, itself a reference to the old jewelry store. On Sundays, Pat, the owner, made a big batch of soup for the coming workweek and made sure to feed John, whom she seemed to regard as a sort of stray.

When John took over the rent at 376½ South Main, the place was packed floor to ceiling with storage from the old owners. The landlord cleared most of it, leaving John with grimy, sprawl-ing open rooms, undraped windows streaming sunlight through the dust. Oddball castoffs were left behind—a metal breadbox that John made into his mailbox; an antique porcelain sign listing shopping staples—bread, salt, flour.

Aside from the street address downstairs, John had no postal designation for his room, so he added it at the front door: Apt. X.

He replaced the flimsy wooden apartment door with a thick steel security door he'd found at a hospital rummage sale, along with some surgical lights that he set up in an attempt to illumi-nate a space that more resembled an indoor basketball court than an apartment.

Perhaps the best amenity of the loft was its roof access. The roof was like an elevated patio, and that's where we'd begun this spring evening: at a cookout three stories above Main Street, open sky above, stunning views of the city all around. From there, we could see across to the Goodrich rooftops and over to the few tall buildings that defined our middling skyline. The glaring-red BJ spire above the newspaper building now served literally as John's personal digital clock, visible from his bedroom window.

With no one to disturb, we played the music loud—Pavement, the Minutemen, the Feelies. John had set up a slide projector in one of his windows and aimed it across Main Street onto the white front of an old furniture store. I sat at the edge of the roof and we watched pictures flash in uneven staccato, a haphazard montage of how we had arrived here, on this perfumed night, under someone else's stars, feeling like the only people in the world.

"Hold it," John rasped suddenly. "Someone's coming!"

We looked down and saw the headlights a block away, creeping forward along the alley. There was no way to get down quickly, and no obvious place to scramble to get ourselves off the back edge of the staircase. I swung my legs over a rusty step, hooking at the knees, and hung there, suspended. My brother looked back at me. The coins fell from my pocket.

"Don't move," he whispered.

John and Larry had shrunk up against the building, but they too had no place to hide.

Within moments, I could see that it was a police car. It moved at a pace nearly as slow as the canal, then stopped when it came up even with the Anthony Wayne. The spotlight locked on John and Larry, then slowly cast upward onto my brother and me. I couldn't see through the car's windows, and the light made it hard to see anything more than its chrome source and the general white shape of the squad car. The beam eased back down to John and Larry, holding for another long moment, then, suddenly, went dark. We heard the click of the gearshift and the car started moving again. We watched as it reached the end of the alley, turned, and disappeared in the fading reds of taillights.

Maybe we weren't worth it. Or maybe he'd decided we belonged there. Or maybe, probably, he just didn't care.

We never did find our way inside that night. There was no obvious entry point, and better judgment had begun to dull the adventure. Imagination would continue to fill all the empty spaces.

ANARCHY GIRLS

They were going the wrong way in the tunnels, and John didn't know what to do about it and I certainly didn't know what to tell him. Anarchy girls were always trouble, and these had arrived from Philadelphia stoned and of a number that was hard to determine because they never held still long enough to count them. Here were two, going off into one of the brick tunnels that led to what could be anywhere, and I almost opened my mouth to ask about the issue of liability, but even where anarchy girls are involved, no guy wants to look that uncool. So I said nothing, but stayed close to John, partly so he knew he had my support as a friend, but mostly because last time I'd been down here in the weak artificial light, I'd heard a great deal of varmintlike scurrying off in the dark corners.

It would be so easy to get lost down here in the underworld, and this was the key difference: the girls seemed to want to get lost and I was doing my best to remember the way back out.

John had discovered the tunnels. For years, we'd heard rumors, legends, that Akron had a vast, complex network of tunnels, connecting factories and other institutions. As the story went, some were for underground deliveries between manufacturing plants and warehouses, some were for access to the massive complex of utility lines and pipes that served the central city. And some were said to have been built for high-stealth, high-stakes security—Akron was considered a top potential domestic target during World War

II, primarily because of the importance of the synthetic-rubber research taking place here. By developing an alternative to the natural rubber whose supply had been cut off by the Japanese, Akron's chemists helped keep the military rolling on tires, floating in rafts, and airborne in blimps and balloons. One expert proclaimed this research so vital that without it "there would have been no Manhattan Project, no Polaris submarine, no man on the moon."

As time went on, John and I heard about more and more of these secret passages. We heard about a tunnel that started under one of the bars and led across the street to St. Vincent Cemetery. We heard about a tunnel from the storied, old hilltop house where Thomas Edison was married to the carriage house behind it. We heard about whorehouses on Howard Street connected by secret passages to the factories. John had actually seen a passage that started with a trapdoor in the ladies'-room floor at a local bar and led under the street to who knew where.

The notion of all these tunnels just below our feet, crisscrossing and meandering, of a world underground, a world darker and richer and fuller of mystery—this is what a child of the industrial Midwest craves. Because it disproved what the wider world wanted to believe—that our place was mundane, without intrigue or romance, that it was uncomplicated, unpoetic.

John had worked his way through college in a small rubber factory, not one of the main ones, but one of the countless others, the oddball places that produced things such as the pigment that makes tire whitewalls white and rubber floor mats and—yes—condoms. There really was a condom factory in town, which, among other things, served to complete the Rubber City joke.

Some of John's coworkers had spent time at the big tire companies, and they told stories about the tunnel systems under the sprawling corporate campuses of Goodyear and Goodrich. The tunnels were the domain of the pipe fitters, who used them to maintain the complex steam and water systems that supported the factories. But, the stories went, the pipe fitters also used them for a sophisticated underground network of drinking, smoking, gambling, and pornography. They set up projectors deep in the tunnels and ran a chauffeur service with their motorized carts, delivering their customers to the show. There, in a smoke-filled catacomb, a group of factory workers who'd stolen away from their machines would sit and watch stag films, drinking, staring into the flickering darkness.

So, yes, of course we wanted this to be true. And now John not only had found a set of these tunnels, but had managed more or less to have them turned over to him to do as he pleased. You could say this had happened by accident, but these kinds of accidents only happen to those who are seeking them. Not long after John and I had broken into the old Goodrich factory, Operation Greengrass had moved closer to fruition: 3.5 million square feet of factories and offices was about to become the biggest vacant lot any of us had ever seen. Its obliteration was such a fait accompli that the makers of a Sylvester Stallone / Wesley Snipes action movie called *Demolition Man* had approached Goodrich, asking if they could blow up one of the old, vacant factories on film. We, being Akronites, had taken this news as flattery: Hollywood had noticed us.

But then, at the eleventh hour, a private investor lured by the two Goodrich attorneys who'd been put in charge of decommissioning the complex had agreed to save it. For what, no one could say.

John knew exactly what to do. He approached one of the attorneys and asked if he could use some of the space for an art studio, which they'd agreed to, and then a gallery, which they'd also agreed to, because when you have that much empty real estate, you'll take in anyone willing to give it life. In this way the big idea that we had always talked about—to prove the worth of the condemned—took hold.

You have to come from a place like this to stake a claim in a decrepit thirty-five-acre brownfield and call it victory. Brownfield—that's what these abandoned factory sites were called, and they were all around us, everywhere we went. John claimed the old Goodrich glazier's shop as his "office." The room sat to the side of an open factory floor.

Soon, as he began to clear out a space for the galleries, John discovered the opening that led into the underground.

I'd been through this passage that led from the gallery area to John's office many times, but it never seemed the same, and I had to navigate carefully when he wasn't there to lead the way. One stretch was too low to walk through upright, causing claustrophobia to gather in its passage; this also raised the question of its function. So now I felt that I knew something these anarchy girls didn't, but I also felt the opposite: maybe they did know what they were doing and maybe I was missing the point. I had felt this way most of my life, and particularly when in the company of free-spirited young women.

"You gotta go back that way," John said resolutely, pointing in the direction of the gallery. "There's nothing down here. And it's dangerous."

One held up her plastic cup, half full of beer, as though in toast to what might have been, and they headed back the way John had directed. He looked at me, shook his head, laughed, and we continued.

John's space was filled with artifacts of its past life, which seemed at once tantalizingly recent and cloudily distant. Clipboards held production schedules, the dates of the pay stubs discovered in desk drawers were not that long before. This aspect of time could be measured in months. But the tire molds and schematics he found suggested a long-gone culture, something measured in eras. Goodrich had an infinity of windows—fiftysome buildings, each with hundreds of panes—so glazier's were a constant necessity of maintenance. John's office was filled with pieces of glass and anachronistic tools that made it seem like a reenactor's set at one of those living museums: the Glazier's Shoppe at Rubberland.

This place was an abandoned shrine to something we couldn't fully comprehend. The sense of recently departed humanity was almost ghostly. John had found snapshots of some of the workers taken as they were out drinking at nearby bars, bars we ourselves had been in with the same attitude of camaraderie, bars like the ones we had left to come here the night before John's wedding. And he had found pieces of their clothing, cigarette lighters, family photos, the fallout of layoff slips that prompted rash exits.

A few of us regarded this state as beautiful. My wife and I had been helping John prepare the galleries and had attended his first show, an event that seemed to capture much of what we hadn't been able to define until then: the possibilities of a place no one else wanted. It seemed like a huge success—a hundred or so people came through this trio of homemade art galleries, which John named the Millworks. It was written about in the newspaper. John managed it all, bringing together something that seemed as relevant as it did unlikely.

For this next show, John had contacted a guy named Scott Moore. The two of them had been in art school together at the University of Akron. Scott had moved to Philadelphia, where he'd become part of a loose-bound art collective squatting on Mascher Street. John's idea was for Scott to organize some of his artist friends into a group show that would fill the three galleries in the old tire complex. The show would be called *Straight Outta Philly*, after N.W.A.'s album *Straight Outta Compton*.

They began haphazardly wandering in on the Thursday before opening weekend, one car and then the next and then another, like the advance guard from folkways unknown. Not one of them—the cars and maybe the people too—looked sound enough to have covered the 350 miles from Philadelphia. One of the first cars expelled a man we would only know by the nickname his physical demeanor immediately suggested—Frankenstein—and he stumbled forward a few steps, turned, dropped his zipper, and urinated where he stood. Two of the anarchy girls flitted from the rear and immediately disappeared into the web of alleys between the smutted brick factories. A battered van arrived, somewhere between bronze and brown, with a plumber's logo on the side— FRANK WOLF COMPANY—and the men from inside became known to John and me as the Company of Wolves.

John had driven to Philadelphia months before and made the arrangements. He was expecting maybe a dozen artists. But they kept coming—twenty, thirty of them, most of whom appeared to have taken this as a late-summer road trip and had little or nothing to do with the show. They unloaded case after case of Joe's beer—a Philadelphia product, thin, pale stuff whose local counterpart, P.O.C. (Pride of Cleveland), was a shared icon—and they took off in various directions as though they were sightseers stepping off the bus at Yellowstone.

The galleries were just inside one of the main iron gates leading into the factory complex, which opened into a brick parking lot / courtyard ringed with buildings. With so much real estate to redevelop, the new owners had concentrated first on the most visible areas, and here they'd leased space to a restaurant owner whose Main Street delicatessen had closed. He'd opened a cavern-ous restaurant and jazz-and-blues club called Satchmo's, which was so nice it seemed doomed to fail. But the Millworks galleries had the prime spot, just inside the main gate. One gallery was called the Shoe Shop because it occupied a small building where Goodrich employees purchased their work shoes and brought them for repair. When he first started clearing out the space, John found random shoes and boots in corners and cubbyholes. The next gallery occupied a long, upward stairwell and landing, with the art hung on the ascending walls. It was called the Big Hand. And the third was another staircase, this one descending, called Zone de Confusion. Every car that entered to go to Satchmo's had to pass the galleries. This was the sentinel.

By the time I arrived Friday evening, the night before the opening, John's usual calm had been replaced by a bad cross of whimsy and thinning patience.

"I've been out all day looking for a fish," he said.

"A fish?" I said.

"Yeah. The guy with the dreadlocks needed a fish."

"What kind of fish."

"A whole one. With the head. And tail."

"You mean a dead one?"

"Yeah."

"Did you find one?"

"Yeah, finally. He was very selective."

"What's he gonna do with it?"

"He's gonna wrap it up and nail it to one of his sculptures."

"Won't it smell?"

John raised his hands halfway and shook his head, disavow-ing any responsibility, as if to say finding this fish was enough and anything beyond that was somebody else's problem or, maybe more to the point, was everyone else's problem, which made it the audience's problem, which made it the problem of Art.

It was hot and sticky and I thought maybe John and I could go into Satchmo's for a beer, but he had to stay and supervise the setup.

Through the window of the Shoe Shop, I could see the *Straight Outta Philly* guys hard at work, installing the show. They all were the kind of dirty that looked permanent. I recognized Scott Moore from his Akron days, broad-shouldered, dressed like a foundry worker in heavy Carhartt work pants and a plain T-shirt, unkempt but conventionally handsome, self-assured. Even more, I recognized his type, from the traveling hard-core bands that used to come through town. There was always a charismatic leader, an anarchist with organizational skills, who attracted the best and worst of whatever subculture he represented. Scott was heavily involved in music and had been in an industrial-noise band called Sink Manhattan, an offshoot of which would be playing at the following night's opening. They were called Lick the Earth. The guy with the fish was the guitar player.

Everything I could see half-assembled in the Shoe Shop was familiar to me: reclaimed steel, rusty, manipulated, welded, and bent. This seemed to be the only kind of art anyone from here was making then, intentionally unglamorous, pulling scraps from industrial sites and hammering them together or apart—whichever direction they hadn't already gone. I knew nothing about how to make art, but I had learned by osmosis how to oxidize copper into green and blue and how to accelerate rust and to abuse aluminum. I had seen a course title in a college catalog—Advanced Metals—and written its name on a slip of paper because I thought it was interesting, the idea of evolution applied to something so elemental. In Akron, rust was a legitimate medium.

John said he needed to get home, to his "safe haven." But he couldn't leave until he had everyone out of the galleries, and the more he tried to create order, the more slippery everyone got. He had agreed to allow Scott and some of the others to sleep in the glazier's shop, but now he was worried about how to separate the responsible nihilists from the irresponsible ones.

Frankenstein wandered by, drinking a beer, seeming not to notice us, seeming to be noticing a lot of things that weren't there, and a menagerie of Philadelphians with bedhead and inside-out clothing came tripping through. Two, both dressed in ragged, homemade cutoffs and thrift-store dress shirts and ties, rode through on bicycles, a parade of freaks leading the way.

There is a kind of late-summer rain in Ohio that builds and builds in pent-up humidity, then comes gushing out in a climactic release that is also incomplete, so that it remains humid even as the sky carpet bombs the earth. The result is something like celebration mixed with apprehension, which is how things always seemed to go here—we could never just cut loose because we knew something would always go wrong. This was not pessimism or superstition, but a justifiable and quantifiable worldview. Annually, for each of the previous three years, we had stood at the verge of climactic victory and watched it all end in mind-boggling, history-making defeat. The Drive, in 1987, bringing a shocking end to what appeared to be a Browns play-off victory. The Fumble, in 1988, doing exactly the same. The Shot, in 1989, a stunning, last-second gut-punch that ended a Cavaliers play-off dream. That's all we understood: the anxiety of having hoped for too much and celebrated too soon.

So the notion of a downpour as a metaphor for release, for deliverance, for abandon, for soul-cleansing—that just doesn't work here. We know better.

And that was precisely the type of rain that began pounding the roof of the old Goodrich complex as my wife, Gina, and I sat with John in his office, the humidity intensifying the lingering smell of machine oil and metal that filled the old factory. Whoever had slept here the night before had left the place a wreck and had written *Lick the Earth* all over everything. For someone such as John, who had gone through art school at a time when the likes of Keith Haring and Jean-Michel Basquiat and Fab 5 Freddy were pulling the contemporary strings of street aestheticism, it was hard to get directly upset about graffiti. But still.

Frankenstein had become the symbol of everything that was happening: bludgeoning, oblivious, wayward, recalcitrant. We'd driven through the main gate to see him drenched, in a striped, button-down shirt, holding a beer cup in one hand, pissing toward a fence, like this night's version of a Buckingham guard. Despite the rain, Lick the Earth had set up its amplifiers and PA system outside, under a brick arch at the entrance gate, with sheets of plastic draped over the speakers. The opening had begun, and John's friends, people he knew from the art community, from school, from work, people we didn't know—they were dashing from the parking lot to the Millworks space with newspapers and umbrellas and shirttails held over their heads as the rain pounded without relent.

The fish had already begun to smell, raising the question of its future: the show was supposed to remain up for six weeks.

Gina and I followed John through the tunnels back to the galleries. We moved outside, close to the action, but under cover of an overhang. Two of the anarchy girls were dancing together out in the rain, streetlights casting them in yellow-black. One had stripped down to her bra. The space around the drum kit and the amplifiers was strewn with heavy chains and lengths of pipe, a battered trombone, and a trumpet. A hulking piece of semicylindrical, rusty steel sat in the center. These were pieces of their sculpture, intended now as living art. The drummer took his place and started a random pattern, and the guitar player and the bass player followed with a low, distorted nonmusical cacophony. Scott took one microphone and a guy in a black T-shirt and cap and a cast on his left arm took the other, and together they started a haunted caterwaul, growling and yelping in indecipherable improvisation. Scott picked up a length of chain and began stalking back and forth, trailed by its steely jangle, then turned and began swinging it against the big steel hunk, its harsh clank arrhythmic to the drums. He threw the chain down and picked up the trombone and began to blow squawks and blasts, holding the microphone in the bell so the sound came out drenched in reverb. Lick the Earth congealed into long, atonal loops, the sound of being boiled alive.

The *Straight Outta Philly* entourage began stalking the perimeter, flailing their arms madly in a dance that seemed interpretive, but of what I couldn't say. They moved out into the rain and seemed intoxicated by it, dancing in stutter steps and long body sways—boys in black T-shirts and tank tops, barefoot, pants rolled up; anarchy girls in peasant dresses and shorts. I couldn't count them, they seemed to merge and divide, merge and divide, rolling around on the slick paving bricks and throwing their hands up into the rain, clustered in groups then wandering off solo.

Cars were passing through the gates, couples and groups of friends out for an evening at Satchmo's. Some accelerated to get past these men swinging their chains and brass horns; others slowed to gape. One driver stopped and began honking his horn, either in protest or harmony, it was hard to say. One of the anarchy girls in a cardigan sweater and skirt began climbing the high iron fence at the entrance and was approached by another, a toothy, voluptuous brunette dressed in a too-small pair of short-

shorts and halter top and a red plastic hard hat. She wore a pair of patent-leather pumps and walked in a perpetual tap dance, her spilling-out breasts bouncing and thick thighs alternating like diesel pistons. She reached up for a crossbar and began to climb too, stopping and swaying back and forth like a caged gorilla.

One of the lawyers who'd given John this space was in attendance, and he came over with a hey-I'm-just-tryin'-to-be-cool-here-but-this-is-a-little-too-much demeanor and asked John if he could keep them off the gate, as though there were some sort of boundary to the chaos and this was it. John approached the gate and told the girls they had to get down, and they slithered off the wrought iron and back into their dance without any direct acknowledgment of the order. The tap dancer skipped and twirled across the parking lot, cutting through the Satchmo's patrons who were dashing through the downpour toward the restaurant's lighted entrance. She took up a spot at the front door of the restaurant, dancing and flapping her arms as people rushed past her to get inside, frightened and confused, looking at her. She dropped to the ground and began rolling in a puddle, ending with her chin propped in her palm and legs crossed behind her, like a chanteuse splayed across a piano bar. The girl in the cardigan swayed wildly among two men who danced with faces up toward the sky, and she stopped suddenly, hands in pockets, as if she'd run out of ideas, gazing blankly for a long moment before dropping into a lineman's stance and rushing at one of the young men.

Scott was chanting something into the microphone as his friend blew long bleats from the trumpet and then grabbed the other mic, and the only words I'd recognized all night as words came tumbling out in a guttural chant:

All this rain is pourin' down!
All this rain is pourin' down!

All this rain is pourin' down!
All this rain is pourin' down!
All this rain is pourin' down!

The literalness of it took me by surprise; it didn't seem possible that any of them was reacting to anything that I could also understand, that there was any logic in the performance.

The girls were up the fence again and John went over calmly and told them to come down. They did. Frankenstein, standing among the onlookers, turned casually toward the brick wall behind them and began to pee again. A young man dressed in rags came bouncing heavily out of the Shoe Shop on a pogo stick made of an industrial spring and welded scrap steel, a piece of sculpture that was supposed to be on display in the gallery, and John tried to wave him back inside, but he just kept going and it appeared that stopping might be dangerous because this—none of this—seemed designed for stopping.

They were all made of liquid now. They would lean forward and squeeze out a shirttail or a long hank of hair and rain would gush out and immediately be replaced by more. The girl in the cardigan came rolling across the brick driveway in front of us and stopped, flat on her back in the rain, resting, and the tap dancer vamped over to Satchmo's door again, holding her hard hat in front of her like a cabaret derby. Scott, grunting in harsh rhythm, threw his microphone down and picked up a thick metal pipe with both hands and began beating against the hunk of steel with all his might, over and over and over until he dropped to his knees, exhausted, and then the man in the cast took up the rhythm with a battleship chain, beating and beating, the drums behind him seeming weak and thin in comparison. Cars continued to pass within feet of them, coming and going, but Lick the Earth never acknowledged them, never acknowledged us, never acknowledged the dancers, never acknowledged one another. There was nothing directly conscious about them, this was all of the gut alone.

I stood with my arm around Gina and saw in her face a reflection of what I was feeling—something like mesmerization. Not appreciation or revulsion or even fascination, but an involuntary submission to the rhythm of what we were observing, which rhythm was something that couldn't be measured except by that look on her face.

I watched Scott, speaking in tongues into the microphone, drenched but somehow not electrocuted, trombone dangling at his side like a missile launcher, and suddenly I resented him and the man with the broken arm and the one who'd put the fish inside and Frankenstein and the anarchy girls and the entire Company of Wolves. I resented them because they were defining what didn't belong to them, what they hadn't earned, and I was afraid they were doing it in a way that couldn't be erased, because I had no answer to what I was hearing and seeing.

This place was supposed to be ours, and we had inherited it the hard way, by discovery and loyalty and perseverance. I didn't want to give it up so easily.

The anarchy girls were climbing the fence again and there was no way to stop them.

John picked me up at my house late the next morning and we made the two-minute drive into downtown. The rain had stopped and everything was muggy again. Gina and I had left before Lick the Earth was done because it didn't seem as if they would ever be done, and John said it had never actually ended but rather died like a bored campfire and he had no idea what time, just that it had died. He'd waited until everyone was outside the galleries and locked the door, didn't offer anyone a place to stay.

As we drove down Main Street toward the Goodrich buildings, we began to see bodies on the sidewalk, one here, one there, random Philadelphians. Some were lying with heads in the crooks of their arms, others wandering zombielike. I don't know what they were looking for, but on a Sunday morning in downtown Akron in those years, they weren't going to find it. Ours would likely be the only car to pass down Main Street for hours. There were more bodies as we got closer, some moving, some not. Frankenstein sat on the sidewalk with his back against the fence at the entrance, one arm draped obliquely across the top of his head. The Company of Wolves were gathering together pieces of random steel, tossing them into the van. They were bloody and dirty and half-dressed, even more disheveled than when they'd begun. The guitar player had his dreadlocks tied up in a plume. The cast on the one guy's arm looked to be damaged. Scott was the only one whose heart seemed to be in the dismantling.

John parked and we went through a back door, into the tunnels, a direction I didn't know, down under the ground, and we emerged at the glazier's room and looked around. There was a mess to clean up. We got to work.

PART FOUR

THE MIDDLE
IS NEAR

YOU KNOW, IT'S FUNNY. YOU COME
TO SOMEPLACE NEW AND EVERY-
THING LOOKS THE SAME.

-EDDIE, *STRANGER THAN PARADISE*

BATTLEGROUND

For six weeks in the late summer and fall of 2004, I traveled the state of Ohio, trying to explain it.

I didn't really think of it that way. I thought I was doing something else. In fact, I don't think this felt like an attempt to "explain" until it was too late. That moment arrived just after dawn on October 15, when the red light on top of the camera in a suburban Cleveland production studio flashed on.

I was sitting alone on a stool facing the square lens, with a monitor showing a feed from the New York studio of *FOX & Friends*. Steve Doocy, one of the cohosts, introduced the segment, introduced me as a columnist for the *Akron Beacon Journal* who had been putting in nearly as many miles on Ohio's highways as the tour buses of George W. Bush and John Kerry, who were criss-crossing the state with such fervor that I'd envisioned them happening randomly into the same Duke & Duchess for a pit stop, reaching simultaneously into the drink cooler . . .

You?!

You?!

Well, at least there's one thing we can agree on—the cool, refreshing kick of Mountain Dew!

Doocy asked the question everybody was asking that fall: Which way is Ohio going to go?

My response began, something along the lines of "Well, you know, it's a lot more complicated than that . . ."

Although I was five hundred miles away, I could feel the wind come out from the anchor team in New York and imagined a producer on the other side of the desk frantically making that slashing motion with his finger across his throat, reaching for one of those giant shepherd hooks. Meanwhile, on my end, the producer in cargo shorts and T-shirt—who if he wasn't wearing a Cleveland Browns stocking cap may as well have been, he being of the styrofoam-cup-of-convenience-store-coffee sort, going about his work with the trademark nonchalance of the jaded cameraman—smirked knowingly.

You said the poison word, he told me.

Complicated? I said.

Yep, he said. Those guys want red, and blue.

There's a regional quirk. Every native of the Rust Belt has heard it. Whenever someone mentions they've moved here from somewhere else, our involuntary response is "Why?"

Not as in "Why would anyone do such a thing?" but rather a genuine, hard-won curiosity. We're used to people leaving. We're not used to people arriving.

We're defensive. We just are. We're so conditioned to being overlooked or misinterpreted or invoked as a punch line that whenever someone else tries to paraphrase us in any way, we bristle. Cleveland was called the Mistake on the Lake for so long that the chip on the shoulder became a kind of beloved appendage. So now the local Great Lakes Brewing Company makes a Burning River ale, taking ownership of one of the city's most embarrassing public moments, when the tragically polluted Cuyahoga River caught on fire. I remember hearing a story once about the local music paper doing a big piece on Chrissie Hynde, the Pretenders singer who always seemed like our overseas ambassador. When arrangements were made for the cover shoot, she said she wanted to be photographed in a T-shirt that was locally popular at the time, with the motto CLEVELAND—YOU GOT TO BE TOUGH written in factory smoke over a gritty cartoon skyline. The editor mailed his own shirt to her address in London because, I think, he understood how important the message is, and specifically our ability to control it.

So, yes. We are defensive. (We get called Iowa a lot. Nothing against Iowa, but that's like being named Jenny and having a guy call you Jessa.)

Therefore, when all of a sudden we find ourselves in control of who will become the leader of the free world, and people all suddenly fix their gaze on us (e.g., April 25, 2004, *New York Times Magazine* cover: "Welcome to OHIO. A Swing State. Pop. 11,435,798"; or, e.g., September 9, 2012, *New York Times Magazine* cover: "Way to Go Ohio: . . . The answer could decide the next presidency") and want to know what makes us tick, we tense up.

The problem isn't so much that Ohio is complicated. Every place is complicated if you apply yourself to trying to understand it. The problem is *how* it's complicated.

I set off early in the morning, headed south. It was late August, the day was hazy, and the heat was rising.

The first stretch of highway took me through the grimy fired-clay center of Akron, a landscape sketched with weedy railroad beds and crooked utility poles and chain-link fences, factories with the windows painted green, trees that always looked lost, prodigal, growing up from beds of rock and caked mud and crumbled asphalt where guardrails stand as empty-property lines.

I passed the imposing, abandoned brick wall of the Akron Brewing Company, its name carved a century before in sandstone set into the brick, a tree growing from the decay in its roof, looming above the highway. One wall after another like this, smoky brick pocked with windowpanes filmy and shattered. And then this morphed into the colorful signage of suburbia, the long stretches of Super Retail and the cattle-call restaurants where everything is grilled to perfection.

And then through Canton, the next urban center, ruddy and overcast. I drove past the world headquarters of Diebold, Inc., which had recently gotten into the business of manufacturing and selling touch-screen voting machines. These machines would transform voting for many Americans, a new technology for an old, inscrutable tradition. Those machines would raise all sorts of questions, all sorts of suspicions. *Somebody must be up to something. Something must be about to go wrong.* This more than anything else seems to be the spirit of the election season.

From there, the highway dissolved into the bucolic Ohio landscape, barns set off into the hills, clusters of horses and cows, long, soft furrows in the earth, the iron-rich intoxication of soybeans, gnarl of feral orchards, pillars of smoke every now and again celebrating an American freedom: to burn piles of rubbish on unincorporated soil.

I stopped at the exit marked NEWCOMERSTOWN, at a McDonald's entirely themed to Cy Young, who is buried nearby in an Amish cemetery; his fanciful monument bearing a winged baseball stands audacious among weathered slabs reading YODER and MILLER. The legendary pitcher is even more roundly memorialized in the fast-food restaurant, with museum boxes and framed memorabilia on the walls, his legend running all the way back to the antiseptic restrooms: a baseball with an indecipherable scrawl, a wool uniform under glass, a plastic action figure, cards and pictures. This was impressive at first, certainly a surprise, but ultimately unsettling. Do we want fast-food restaurants to double as repositories of culture? Maybe we do.

Then, soon, I entered a forest. Mile after mile it grew darker and greener, a dense tunnel of trees, winding farther and farther south, Wayne National Forest, covering 241,000 acres.

And that expelled me into my destination, Athens, the home of Ohio University, which traditionally comes in near the top of rankings of the nation's most noteworthy party schools, a town cut off from the rest of civilization, richly scented with patchouli and greasy onions and last night's beer, a place where the baby-boom generation's idealists can still believe in possibility because they live inside a forest, a place where chapbooks are published and read. My most significant personal connection to Athens was the number of friends and acquaintances I knew who'd been arrested there on Halloween, an Ohio rite of passage.

In a way (okay, completely), I was there for a cheap joke: in the county that is well-known as Ohio's party headquarters, I was planning to compare Athens's two party headquarters—Republican and Democrat. This was hardly a fair comparison. Athens is an anomaly in the midst of Appalachia, a liberal college town awash in Day-Glo and cappuccino and daddy's credit limit. A truer destination might have been the nearby Hocking College, which offers courses in lumberjacking, and where some students arrive for class on horseback. But because Athens-the-college-town dominates Athens-the-county demographically and philosophically (Democrats had outnumbered Republicans 9,214 to 2,632 in that year's primary election), visiting the political-party offices offered a dramatic contrast to explore.

I followed the address for the Democratic headquarters to a storefront next door to a burrito house with a sign proudly stating WORKER-OWNED, and whose bill of fare included tofu fajitas. In late morning, the town was mostly asleep in the way only a college town sleeps, its sidewalks stained and littered with the previous night's activity, a heavy atmosphere of metabolisms at a simmer.

A young man in a baseball cap and loose shorts sat drowsily on the headquarters' doorstep, waiting for a bus. Otherwise, no one was outside.

The door was locked. The storefront windows were plastered with two dozen campaign signs. Peering past them, I could see a frat-house clutter of telephone lines, computer wires, pizza boxes, bumper stickers, and cardboard cartons askew in the aisles. Later, when I was allowed inside, I saw, on a desk, a handwritten thank-you note from Al Franken to the Democratic Party chairwoman. Even though it was early in the season, pre–Labor Day, young volunteers were constantly coming and going, picking up campaign materials, stopping in for information, chatting, eager, hopeful, certain.

Later that day, I made my way out to the Republican headquarters, in a strip plaza at the outskirts of town. It hadn't yet officially opened. There was only one phone line, compared to eight at the Democratic office. It could probably best be described as "broom clean." The party chairman's air of resignation was hard to miss. Parked next to his SUV, with its SPORTSMEN FOR BUSH bumper sticker, was a car with a KERRY/EDWARDS sticker.

The answer is always in the journey, rather than its destination. It was not Athens, but rather the road to Athens, and the road that would continue for weeks, that illuminated why it was so difficult for me to answer "Whither goes Ohio?" Not because I didn't know (although I didn't), but because the question itself was too simple. In just this one leg of my campaign, I'd passed through major manufacturing centers, deeply rooted farm country, a national forest, gaudy suburbs, a third-world Appalachia that most Americans can't fathom.

Which way is Ohio going?

The answer is "Which Ohio?"

*   *   *

Just outside Cincinnati, I pulled into the auxiliary parking area across the road from St. Ignatius Catholic Church. The church's vast parking lot was full, much of it occupied by the tents and carnival rides of the parish's summer festival, the rest by rows of cars belonging to those attending the event. I parked on a baseball field, under a billboard with the words IN GOD WE TRUST. UNITED WE STAND over an American flag.

On the drive here, I'd been scanning radio stations: Christian rock . . . Christian hip-hop . . . Christian sports talk. I had never heard an all-Christian sports-talk station before, nor, as far as I can recall, even considered the genre. But here it was, and like all mainstream entertainment prefaced by Christian, it sounded exactly like the secular version, only with a highly tangential cast to the content—kind of like biting into a jelly doughnut to find it filled with peanut butter. The discussion that day involved the skimpy outfits worn by the Olympic beach-volleyball players and the larger issue of whether Christian athletes felt compromised by being forced to wear tight, immodest attire. Swimmers in swimsuits and whatnot.

Which is to say that, culturally, Cincinnati is distinctly different from the rest of the state. It's a river town, the beginning of the American South, the top edge of the Bible Belt, a highly conservative city whose modern reputation was forged in many minds by the 1990 censorship controversy over Robert Mapplethorpe's homoerotic photographs exhibited at the Cincinnati Contemporary Arts Center.

The event I'd come for was called Igi-Fest, named for the church's patron saint, and celebrated across a sprawling blacktop spread with children's bouncy toys and funnel-cake stands and vats of melty cheese and a game called Chippy Pot. I wandered for a long time, without approaching anyone, just trying to absorb it, to find a focus, an entry point. Throughout this whole process I had been trying actively, consciously, probably neurotically, to avoid presumption. It's the native instinct in a place that's been plagued by presumption. When you live in something called a flyover state, you recoil at even the slightest hint of pigeonholing.

I once was introduced to Ira Robbins, a New York rock critic whom I greatly admired. He asked where I was from and I said, "Akron," to which he responded without hesitation, "Oh, I'm sorry." I'd grown so accustomed to such exchanges that I skipped over anger and went straight to disappointment over the remarkable ease with which he'd exposed his own stupidity.

So, while I had come to this event knowing it reflected a prevailing Christian conservatism in Cincinnati, I wanted to try to get under that surface, or to circumvent it completely, and I knew enough about the gathering process to know that it's better to get ahold of nuance and contrasts and complexities and contradictions before the conversation begins than to try to extract them once the transaction is under way.

So I literally circumvented, just walking around the outside edge of the crowd, watching. What arose from the chaos of activity was a strong prevailing impression of families, of course—the white, middle-class families of Ohio and the wider region, conveying a nuclear, traditional demeanor of wholesomeness and politeness, entirely sincere and elemental. Golf shirts and department-store denim shorts, softball-league manners, and keg beer in moderation. What I found in greatest abundance in Cincinnati and pretty much everywhere else I went was a polite reticence, even among the most ideologically driven of the people I encountered. Often, people didn't readily reveal their party affiliation or which candidate they favored. It didn't seem to be out of suspicion or fear so much as my father's long-standing Thanksgiving instruction: "No religion or politics at the dinner table."

So the first two people I talked to at Igi-Fest, a pair of sisters in their seventies named Esther and Joan, responded coyly when I asked if I could talk to them about the upcoming election. Because my purpose was to try to understand the people behind the votes, I always began open-ended and never directly asked about the campaign or the candidates. But that didn't matter because people just assumed that's what I was after. I couldn't blame them.

Esther, winking, said, "We *know* who *we're* voting for." As the conversation continued, they carefully referred to "our man" and "the other side" without naming names.

However, they also told me they both worked at a Republican phone bank, soliciting volunteers. And that they'd recently attended a George Bush rally. So their position wasn't hard to figure out. Still, I was charmed by the way they maintained this sense of reservation, that they felt their vote was personal, that maybe they even didn't want to offend me in case I was on "the other side."

As I worked my way deeper into the festival, I found, amid booths labeled ICE CREAM and ROULETTE, a tent that sported the sign RELIGIOUS INFORMATION. The husband-and-wife team working a table inside offered me a pamphlet titled "Voter's Guide for Serious Catholics."

This guide, without endorsing any particular candidate or party, contained what could only be described as a mathematical formula for choosing a political candidate, offering five "nonnegotiable issues" and the Church's position on each: abortion, euthanasia, fetal stem-cell research, human cloning, and homosexual marriage. (I found it curious, considering the urgency of Iraq and Afghanistan and the Catholic principle of peace, that war was not included.)

Following the five nonnegotiables, under the heading "How to Vote," the guide explained how to apply each of these issues:

First, determine where each candidate stands on each of the five main points. Then "eliminate from consideration candidates who are wrong on *any* of the nonnegotiable issues."

Once that process is complete, the voter can choose freely from any candidates who pass this test. If there are no acceptable candidates, "you may vote for the candidate who takes the fewest [wrong] positions . . . or you may choose to vote for no one."

Applying a corollary formula, Hamilton County, which Cincinnati dominates, had voted for the Republican candidate in each of the previous six presidential elections; Cincinnati has a strongly conservative identity; ergo, Cincinnati is "red."

Unless you ask the ever-unfolding question: Which Cincinnati?

The following evening, a few miles away, I went to another Cincinnati festival, the final night of a three-day punk and metal marathon at a combination rock club / Laundromat called Sudsy Malone's. (According to the ads: "You can do laundry, get drunk and see live music all in the same building!")

The first message I encountered was scrawled above a men's-room urinal:

I'm worried about the economy.

The second message came from the doorman, a squintily gregarious twenty-five-year-old with a bull ring through his septum and those wide, earlobe-stretching rings that always give me the willies. He had a lot to say (he was definitely antiwar), but had to shout above a band called End It All. His name was Tom and he had a two-year-old daughter and lived with his mother, and he told me he thought the upcoming presidential election would be "like voting for Lucifer or voting for one of his lesser demons."

Which rang oddly in light of the Christian voting pamphlet, because theoretically a staunch believer who calculated "zeros" for two opposing candidates might make the same harshly rigid judgment as Tom, using precisely the same hell-and-brimstone language, even though this imagined voter would be perceived as Tom's cultural opposite.

I left Cincinnati less certain about a lot of things but much more interested in the uncertainty.

I got a bad case of poison ivy once when I was in college. Every person I mentioned this to had a surefire remedy. Baking soda. Calamine lotion. Jewelweed. Bleach. Hot water. Each of these people spoke with such conviction that I couldn't be certain which was the right choice. (An aside: Don't try the bleach thing. Especially if you've already been scratching a lot. Seriously. Just . . . don't.)

A similar bit of the American nature plays out in Ohio every four years. Some swear that if it rains on Election Day, the advantage goes to the Republicans. That a candidate who can swing just ten votes in every Ohio precinct will be guaranteed the presidency. A colleague at the *Cincinnati Enquirer* told me his editors were toying with the theory that they could scrutinize demographic data so closely as to pin down the *one* undecided Ohio voter whose ballot would swing the state and thus the nation.

Canton, twenty minutes south of Akron, sees a quadrennial media pilgrimage, as some analysts swear Canton is the quintessential "typical" city in America, and thus, if you can suss out its mood, you can accurately predict the national outcome.

The editor of Canton's newspaper, the *Repository*, has referred to this as the "Winerip effect," after *New York Times* reporter Michael Winerip moved his family to Canton in 1996, became an actual citizen, and filed a series of insightful and refreshingly nuanced dispatches under the title "An American Place."

The Amish man told me a joke:

"A traveling pollster knocked on old Eli Hershberger's door and asked who he was voting for in November."

"'I don't vote,' Eli said. 'But I *pray* Republican.'"

The Amish man didn't smile when he told the joke nor laugh at the punch line.

And he didn't tell it to me because he was enjoying my company. He didn't want to talk to me at all. He was only doing it because he knew I'd get it wrong if he didn't.

In truth, even though they often claim otherwise, and even though the entirety of their arm's-length-from-mainstream-society public image (with special emphasis on church/state separation) would suggest the opposite, the Amish do vote. Probably in far greater numbers than we know. They're just very, very private about it. Just as they are about pretty much everything else.

The largest concentration of Amish in the United States is less than an hour from Akron, in Holmes County, Ohio, and its surrounding areas. I'd driven there on an early-autumn day, easing instinctively off the accelerator as I left the main highway, flattened turds on the roadway always being a signal to slow down. It's never long before you come across a square, black buggy clip-clopping along the edge of the road. Some of these drivers have attached triangular, orange safety reflectors to the backs of their vehicles, some have not. It depends on how strict they are about their distance from secular society, and from the rules thereof. They call us "the English." Some tolerate us more than others.

For someone like me, who lives in the city, who has always lived in the city, who thinks city, this stretch beyond my borders had always been an inspiration. Entering this part of the state in the fall, as the leaves are changing and the earth is releasing the perfume of its postseason spice of harvest, the air infused with intoxicating, hyperbaric oxygen and nitrogen and an infinity of reds—it felt like another universe. One of the things I love about Ohio (and in great part because this is the opposite of the prevailing outside perception) is how radically diverse it is. Less than one hour in any direction from my house, I can be in a vast acreage of soybean fields that stretch to Iowa, or on the shore of one of the largest bodies of water in the United States that leads to Canada, or in one of the most malignant postindustrial regions in the country that stretches far to the north and east, or in the heart of the nation's Amish culture.

I began my tour with the Amish equivalent of low-hanging fruit, in Sugarcreek, a touristy, shopping-friendly village with a quaintly stylized motif—the Little Switzerland of Ohio—and a constant flow of tour buses, usually carrying retirees with cameras and discretionary cash.

The cameras are unwelcome. Amish people generally do not like having their pictures taken, but are also highly nonconfrontational, so sometimes crass insensitivity goes unchecked. A common sight on these roadways is an amateur photographer parked off to the side, aiming a camera at a bearded farmer driving horses across a field, the farmer trying to crane his face away from the lens while simultaneously keeping an eye on his team.

The cash is not unwelcome. Sugarcreek is neatly lined with shops that sell Amish rocking chairs and wooden Amish pull toys and Amish cookbooks and Amish woven rugs and little souvenir Amish-boy hats and little souvenir Amish-girl bonnets and heavy loaves of Amish bread and Amish rabbit hutches and Amish quilts and Amish whirligigs and DVDs about the Amish and little wooden boxes that just seem so . . . Amish. Moving beyond this orderly commercial center, stretches of road are stripped with banners and signs and sidewalk displays, and it is impossible not to regard it as a woven and wooden version of the dense suburban commercial strips along the interstates. (Serious shoppers can obtain an Amish Passport, which is like a preferred-customer discount card.)

Farther into the country, where clothes hang drying between trees and fading white houses without electrical wires stand amid chicken coops and low silos, homemade signs are propped at driveways and intersections, their block letters advertising eggs and apples and lop-eared rabbits.

The balance of all this is not unlike the balance of a place like Ohio against the larger America—always as complex as it is tenuous.

I once interviewed David Kline, a well-respected Amish author of books on nature and farming. His books are widely distributed, he has been reviewed (quite favorably) in the nation's major newspapers, embraced by the likes of Wendell Berry and Barbara Kingsolver, and he was unreservedly open to being interviewed. But to set up the conversation, I had to mail him a letter making the request, then await receipt of his return letter, which instructed me to call him at an appointed date and time on the community telephone that he shared with his neighbors, which was outside, in a common space. This convoluted arrangement preserves a delicate philosophy to resist technology, to preserve a lifestyle and an ideology and a set of values by a people who are rigid in their beliefs but not at all didactic about them. And it upholds a certain practicality, that the phone can be used as a tool, but its use should be considered, always considered. It's kind of awesome to someone like me who comes from a highly self-conscious culture where doing things the hard way is the highest ideal.

The Amish code is the closest thing I've ever encountered to the punk ethic. I came of age playing music in the underground rock culture of the 1980s. Almost everything I believe ethically and even morally either derives from that experience or was reinforced there. If you have ever rolled around on a basement floor soaked with beer and sweat at an all-ages show, amid swinging arms and stomping feet, you understand the entirely practical implications of "democracy" and "personal responsibility."

A code, an ethic, among the strictest adherents approached something like a religion, complete with ritualistic tattoos, symbolic hairstyles, and strict rules of dress. (No stonewashed jeans, of course. But also no shiny leather or overt hats or other such indication of having considered "style." Even though most of us spent inordinate percentages of our waking hours considering our appearance, and how to groom it in such a way as to seem we'd never given it any thought at all. Such studied nonchalance is pretty exhausting. That's why hipsters are so skinny. They burn a lot of calories trying to look as if they couldn't care less.)

The hierarchy of the local punk-rock scene tended to break down by hairstyle. Skinheads, by virtue of what they had sacrificed for their art (i.e., hair), represented the supreme leadership. Anyone with a socially risky novelty haircut (Mohawk, dreads, etc.) operated on the level of a high diplomat and usually got asked to be in other bands. The rest of us accepted our role as semi-insiders and tried to hide that we had middle-class parents and middle-class haircuts and middle-class futures and also a battery-operated, plug-in guitar tuner. Any outward suggestion of musicianship or ambition was suspect.

In similar fashion, devout Amish men stop cutting their beards and women grow their hair long after marriage, a symbol of their maturing in their commitment. (In 2011, a group of Amish radicals, in a series of attacks on peers whom they considered untrue to the Church, violently hacked off their victims' beards and hair. The ringleader of these attackers, it's worth mentioning, had the last name Mullet.)

In the Akron-Cleveland scene, the skinheads were the opposite of the aggressive, often-racist skinheads in other cities. Ours were basically hippies without the hair or the drugs. They were all pacifists. Some were vegetarians. Many were straight-edge, with black X's drawn (or sometimes even tattooed) on their wrists indicating they didn't drink or smoke or get high. The most austere of these also abstained from sex, although it's hard to say whether that was by choice. The purest of them all, a soulful, organic guy named Jimi Imij, embraced his ancestral Sioux culture so that he made traditional jewelry and knew the dances and lived in a commune of sorts, a punk-rock flophouse behind the hospital. I became fascinated with Jimi because he seemed heroically idealistic—the first genuinely indigent person I'd ever known, and who seemed to have chosen the condition as a moral imperative—and also because he reminded me of one of my fictional heroes, James Fenimore Cooper's Natty Bumppo, wearing Levi's shredded to fringe and living by a code I couldn't begin to understand. Jimi made something out of everything he found. As far as I could tell, he had never purchased anything in a store. He was always piecing together jewelry on the coffee tables in the rented houses where he flopped, working with serious intent in darkened living rooms crawling with cats and smelling of Bugler tobacco and hobo stew. Jimi would come across abandoned shoes and collect them, so that when I went to visit him, he'd offer me a pair of moldy combat boots from a box in the basement. My brother and I used to joke that if Jimi had a guitar—which he didn't because of his self-inflicted, semitranscendent poverty—it would be made of dirt. Years later he finally did have a guitar. He showed it to me; he had made it out of a piece of driftwood that had washed up from Lake Erie.

At first, Jimi was a fascination. For a while, as I was undergoing my sometimes awkward postcollege entry into something like a traditional middle-class indoctrination, I wondered if he was avoiding his own such transition. But now—and I still see him often—I respect him deeply as a pure soul. He has evolved, yet remains committed to his old ideals, the same ones that informed me. Sleeping on the floors of musicians' apartments in other cities and giving them a floor to sleep on in your own, sharing a drum kit, catching someone who gets knocked asunder in the mosh pit, splitting the door money evenly—these mature into lessons of generosity, of tolerance, of charity. I feel a strong, old connection to Jimi. We understand each other. We live differently, but we return to a shared culture.

Now middle-aged, Jimi is Amish in the same way that an old-order Mennonite is punk rock. Both wear big, black boots. Both maintain highly symbolic hair. Both have chosen their path deliberately, knowing full well there are easier paths to have chosen.

I've heard others accuse the Amish of hypocrisy. They're criticized because they shun the conventions of mainstream society yet market their wares aggressively. They will not own or drive cars, but will allow themselves to be driven in other people's vehicles. They eschew pleasures of the flesh yet allow for a spell of adolescent hedonism called Rumspringa.

The opposite of that criticism is to admire the extent to which they maintain their traditions and convictions despite a society in which this is nearly impossible. The Amish man who told me the voting joke, for instance, allowed himself to be photographed, but only from a discreet distance, and in silhouette, without turning his face to the camera.

I spent a long afternoon talking with an old-order Amish man who owned a furniture shop.

He had no electricity or telephone in his home, but allowed both in his office. No electric lights in the workshop, but gas lights were allowed.

His thirty-four Amish employees couldn't drive or own cars, but were picked up each morning by passenger van.

He can't own a television or computer but told me he'd watched FOX News that morning on a laptop owned by one of his drivers.

A Trans Am was for sale at the end of his driveway, out near the road, and when I asked about it, he hedged at first, then asked me not to include it in my newspaper story. It belonged to his son, he explained in a tone that suggested he wished this high-concept simple life of his were easier.

But he was trying.

His shop makes furniture to a high standard of craft, and without the relative ease of fully modernized production. People buy it in great part because they recognize and respect the reputation of Amish workmanship. It's a mark of quality.

One of the greatest challenges, he told me, has been coming recently from overseas. Imported furniture, mass-produced with cheap labor in Asia, then stamped AMISH MADE, is sold in the same places where his is sold. But with a much higher profit margin. Even to him, and even on close inspection, it's hard to tell the real Amish products from the knockoffs.

This tension carries over into the notion of casting a vote, which is one of the ways Americans are privileged to feel a relief from certain tensions, feel some sense of power or control.

The usual estimate is that fewer than 10 percent of the Amish vote, but this man—who follows news and public opinion closely in his own delicate process—told me he believed the Amish voter turnout would be much higher, probably closer to 40 percent. Most of those votes would be cast absentee. Discreetly.

I continued into October—south to a county full of dead coal mines with a 27 percent poverty rate and then west to a farming community where, in the 2000 election, 74 percent of the presidential votes had gone to George Bush. And then north, to an inner-city Cleveland precinct where, in that same election, *zero* people had voted for Bush.

And then to Columbus, the state capital and the center of Ohio politics, a city so political that drinking establishments are described not as "biker bars" or "gay bars," but rather "Democrat bars" and "Republican bars," a city so political that—I guess I should have seen this coming—no one would talk openly to me about politics. Even the guy selling flowers from a street cart was guarded. It was all too much of a game. Somebody could be listening. Everyone was thinking three steps ahead. They wanted me to play along. That was the only way in.

I left.

Finally, I went to a town I'd never visited before but had always wanted to, a mile from the Indiana border, a town whose name I'd circled on the map way back before I began this long exploration: Hicksville. I went there for the opposite of the cheap joke. I went there for something other than an easy answer. I went there because every four years Ohio comes under this national lens, and I suspect the coastal media forces, and the consumers of that media, sometimes regard us collectively as their own personal Hicksville.

It was now just a few weeks till Election Day. As everyone had predicted, Ohio had evolved from being a battleground state to being *the* swing state. Everybody knew this. We knew it. It was exciting in some ways, and it also made us nervous. Partly because of the louder and louder whispers dreading the specter of becoming "another Florida." Mostly because there were too many ways to get it wrong.

So my purpose in Hicksville was to undermine the shorthand, to look at this place the way I'd looked at all the others, to allow people to speak, to challenge my own perceptions, etc. But a strange thing happened there as I finished a club sandwich in the Sunrise Café and approached the table full of retirement-age, midafternoon coffee drinkers, whom I'd been eavesdropping on during my lunch. I introduced myself, said I'd been traveling the state to write about the election, and they spontaneously, spiritedly, one by one, picked it up from there, responding in a way that seemed completely natural, as though they'd been expecting me, and completely unnatural, because, why would they have been expecting me?

Man #1: "I have voted Independent; I've voted Democrat; I've voted Republican. And I'm a Bush guy."

Man #2: "I'm for Bush."

Woman #1: "Me too."

Man #3: "Put this in your paper—Bush is gonna win."

Then all four turned toward their friend at the adjacent table, a man wearing a hat with the word ROGUE across the front. He shrank back in mock defensiveness.

"I'm a Kerry guy," he said.

But I'd never asked them how they were voting. All I'd said was that I was writing about the election and they'd taken over from there, as though they'd been conditioned by the ubiquity of media to categorize themselves. Maybe they understood what I was after better than I understood it myself. Steve Doocy, the FOX anchor, might agree with that assessment. Maybe I was trying to hard.

What I was after was where we are in agreement. Not long before, I'd spent a day with an apple farmer in northwest Ohio, talking about all sorts of things, one of the best conversations I'd had in a season full of excellent conversations. We were well past lunch before we ever got around to the specifics of this election and his vote. On this warm and generous Ohio autumn day, drunk with bees and plump with squash, the kind of day we acknowledge as the dividend for our investment in an unruly climate, he'd shown me the gorilla costume he keeps in one of his barns ("I just always wanted one") and poured me a glass of unpasteurized cider to demonstrate (convincingly, I'd say) why less government makes for more delicious apple juice. He'd described the corn maze he makes for visiting children each fall. Then he asked if I wanted to see his corn cannon.

We went into a cluttered barn and he rooted around and pulled out a bazooka-like contraption made from two hunks of PVC pipe with an air compressor hookup, self-invented and homemade, the kind of thing farmers do just because they can. He carried it outside into the blue afternoon and dragged an air hose over and hooked it up.

"Wanna try?" He offered the cannon.

I took it in both arms and he explained how to get it balanced and where to aim. Then he tossed a dried hunk of corncob down the five-foot length of pipe and let the pressure build inside the chamber.

I let the barrel rest against my hip and eased the front end toward the sky.

"Ready?"

The farmer squeezed the trigger, and with a resounding *THOOP!* the corncob blasted out, clearing the county highway, arcing across the cerulean sky, spinning and tumbling, wild and free, finally landing in the next acre, announcing its completion with a distant, little plume of dust.

I looked back and he was smiling and he didn't even have to ask. He grabbed another corncob and tossed it down the pipe.

DEMOLITION

This was most definitely the first time I had requested *permission* to get inside the Bank. For all the times I'd been in there, I'd never actually asked. I'd snuck in underage. I'd tried to break in through the old hotel. I'd walked right through the door as though I belonged. For a while there in the beginning, I thought I needed permission. I've come to realize, though, that elitism doesn't work well in places like this. Excluding people is a bad idea when you don't have that many to begin with.

So the fact that I was asking meant either that I had changed, or that something else had changed.

Probably both.

The Bank and the adjacent hotel had been boarded up for more than a decade. All those years, whenever I passed by, I felt, more than anything else, a weird sense of ownership, as if it were partly mine because I had been there when no one else wanted it. A time-share in a ghost hotel. Meanwhile, the city had been clawing its way back from its worst years. The Bank, the Hotel Anthony Wayne, and the surrounding, abandoned buildings were about to be torn down to make way for a minor-league baseball stadium. The Cleveland Indians' AA affiliate would play there. The stadium was to be called Canal Park because the canal that ran behind it was also being reclaimed. Mile by mile, a walking trail was being developed along its length. Since that dynamite explosion in 1913, the canal had continued to exist without context, incongruous, and now a new context was being applied. The following spring—1997—the stadium would open, and an entire corridor of restaurants, bars, new businesses, and housing would follow.

In the industrial Midwest, we tend to describe places not by what they are, but by what they used to be.

So I went to a college with dorms called "the old Holiday Inn," and an art building called Van Devere, after the name of the Pontiac dealership that used to occupy it. The old Quaker Oats grain silos, one of the city's defining features, had been converted into round hotel rooms, the Quaker Hilton.

It seemed appropriate, then, that when Cleveland Browns owner Art Modell covertly sold the team to Baltimore, abandoning us, that the prevailing outcry was to let us keep the team name. It's not so much the idea of clinging to the past as it is a deep understanding that progress is not linear, and the beginning is just as important as what follows. In cities where things were made, we understand the notion of cycles, the way things are worked and reworked, the way excess is gathered from the floor and used for the next job, the way things change and improve, but never completely untie from their origins.

Therefore, when so many physical places were emptied out and left behind, there was constant intrigue in their past, even when they were desolate and even when they were abused, and then later, when they were reclaimed.

Soon after the Bank closed, I started playing in a band, in little rock clubs, and almost every place bands like mine played in was some version of this—a cast-off, a hand-me-down, a curb-find, the architectural equivalent of a thrift-store acquisition. In Akron, in Cleveland, in Pittsburgh, in Youngstown, music centered mainly in bars that had been pulled from the junk heap or fashioned from abandoned warehouses and storefronts. (And almost exclusively, for some reason, at the bottom or top of a steep, cramped staircase, which made the hauling of amplifiers a Sisyphean chore. Everyone who has ever played in a rock band in the Midwest knows this: it is always three in the morning, and it is always snowing, and you're always in a tow-away zone, and there are always stairs.)

I played on a stage with a stripper pole in the middle and on one with abandoned disco lights in its floor and in old movie theaters and a deserted frat bar. Without realizing it, my instincts were being tuned. Eventually, I would establish my family in a forlorn house that was facing condemnation.

I loved wrecked and abandoned buildings not out of a morbid fascination or a sense of exploitation, but because they felt like home.

So in my role as an *Akron Beacon Journal* reporter, I called the city building department and asked if I could get inside the Bank to look around and was given surprisingly easy access. A pre-demolition crew was working there and I could go in anytime during the day, the man said. Try not to get hurt. It felt kind of like the doorman giving a cursory glance to my obviously fake ID.

I went there on a fall afternoon. The façade still looked exactly as it had when I was eighteen, with its name still above the door—THE BANK—in block letters, serifed like the name of a Western saloon. I went through an opening in the back, a way in I didn't know existed, and slowly entered the vast, open room. The cavernous space was filled with murky, indirect light. I'd never been in here in the daytime, and that was the first thing that felt strange—a bar in the daytime that's no longer a bar offers rarefied disorientation—but soon enough *everything* felt strange, changed completely. At the far end of the room was where the stage should have been, but it was gone. So was the parachute that used to hang from the ceiling. The ornate millwork up there was all punched with holes. Plaster crunched underfoot. The bar was gone. The balcony railing was gone. There was no furniture, no shelving or mirrors. The art deco lightshades that used to hang from the ceiling were gone. The only thing left was the huge steel vault door, which had always felt like the building's anchor and still did. I wanted to feel nostalgic, or sad. I think I insisted on feeling that way, and for a minute or so I tried to force it, the way you try to allow tears at an uncle's funeral but find that they won't come. I remembered where I sat that night when the Generics played. I walked straight to the spot, or about where I thought it was. I shifted my weight from one foot to the other. I found it interesting to be inside, certainly. But this was little more than a game. I was in the shell of a life that no longer existed except inside me.

I wanted to tell someone this, but there was no one to tell. A few men in hard hats were outside the doorway, but they wouldn't have cared. All my adult life, I'd been semiconsumed with this notion of who I was and whom I was supposed to become, and only then was I coming to realize that circumstances had filled in the blanks. I was born into a place and time that needed me. That's who I was: a product of all this.

A few weeks later, on a Saturday morning, a crowd gathered a block away, held back by a police barrier. Jimi Imij was there, holding a video camera, which itself seemed science-fictional, a caveman discovering technology, and led me to wonder if he'd fashioned it from beads and kindling. His hair was long and stringy, a baboon ass of baldness at the crown where once he'd shaved strange shapes. Jimi had become a self-made, oddball historian, starting a loose collective called the Ohio Hystairical Musick Society—acronym OHMS (appropriately, the measure of resistance)—gathering up memorabilia of Ohio's music history, all these scattered pieces of a hard-to-assemble past. He'd learned how to burn CDs on a borrowed machine and cobbled together homemade compilations with taped-paper sleeves, giving them away for free. Now he stood amid the crowd on Main Street.

An amplified voice counted down to one, and then, with a loud explosion the back end of the building, behind the old bank, imploded, toppling breathlessly into a cloud of dust, creating a perfect void. But the main section, the Bank and the Hotel Anthony Wayne, remained.

"That big son of a bitch is still standing there!" someone said.

"I guess they put the charge down in the vault," someone else said.

"Hey—put somebody in there that can do it!"

Before the words had a chance to find a hold, another charge boomed and the second half of the building followed the first, disappearing in a billowing cloud. A hole was there so suddenly it took the very breath.

With the building of the stadium—whose redbrick architecture unambiguously reflected that of a factory tower—a momentum of reclamation began. Soon my job at the newspaper became, more or less, to go into these old places and see what they were becoming. I toured an old building with a warren of rooms upstairs, a boardinghouse/brothel that (so the story said) had housed a speakeasy in the basement. It was becoming a bar and restaurant. I explored the ceiling of the old Civic Theater from above, an ingenious gray plaster honeycomb that I viewed from a catwalk that surrounded it. I went through a former Goodyear factory whose closing had destroyed an underpinning of identity and pride, but which had since been reinvented as Goodyear's research and technical center.

And I took one last walk through the old Goodrich factory, the big one at the corner, the one John and I had gone exploring in. The building was being converted into the headquarters of a polymer research firm that was moving to Akron. Polymers are first cousins to rubber, and the idea of the old tire factory's being repurposed for a new form of the old story—and bringing jobs into a place that had lost so many of them—offered a form of hope. Nothing is simple, however, nothing is easy, we certainly know that here. But for that very reason, we are experts at knowing hope when we see it, and for accepting it with the proper caution. Hope here is like an offered stick of cartoon dynamite posing as a cigar.

The center of each floor had been cut out inside the thick concrete pillars to create an atrium that went all the way up to the roof, to let in the light. The edges of the cuts were left exposed, and although concrete is man-made, it has the character and beauty of natural stone, exhibiting strength and ingenuity. (In all these old factories, if you look closely at the ceilings, you can see the grain of the plywood forms into which the concrete was poured. This gives the effect of a fossil, of seeing the organic evolution of the place.) All the graffiti had been sandblasted, but a group of University of Akron photography students had first been allowed to go through and document it on film.

None of this felt like a victory. We'd been in recession, more or less, since the year I'd graduated high school. The population was still receding. Three of the city's four major tire companies had been purchased by foreign competitors, their world headquarters uprooted and moved to other places. Only Goodyear remained, along with the research wing of what was now Bridgestone/Firestone. All of which meant that we were something different that we still couldn't quite put a name on. But it also meant we hadn't given up.

This place has never been defined by success anyway, even when things were at their best. It's always been more about how we deal with failure.

DO NOT CRY FOR ME, ARIZONA

Remember how, on *M*A*S*H*, whenever a character would leave the show, the casting director would pull off a brilliant replacement, a new ensemble member who served a parallel function, but in totally different guise? So Hawkeye Pierce's trusty sidekick Trapper John McIntyre became Hawkeye Pierce's trusty sidekick B. J. Hunnicutt, and commanding officer Henry Blake became commanding officer Colonel Sherman T. Potter, and buffoonish foil Frank Burns became buffoonish foil Charles Emerson Winchester III.

That's kind of what my adult life looks like.

Just about every time I make a new friend or get a good boss or find a decent barber, that person leaves, and then another traipses along, and then that one leaves, and then another, and so on. Every space between is filled with a particular kind of hope, one outfitted with a trapdoor, as though any of these departures could in equal measure represent the final episode or the bridge to the next. I guess that's just the nature of a place whose population has been in steady decline my whole life. I'm in a grudge match with arithmetic.

A century ago, Akron was, briefly yet conspicuously, celebrated as the fastest-growing city in America, a vibrant industrial success. The story goes that a 1920-ish *Los Angeles Times* editorial wistfully mused, *Perhaps one day Los Angeles can become the Akron of the West!*

Like most Eastern and Midwestern factory cities, the place ballooned in the two World Wars, working through the growth spurts of immigration and fat money, developing company neighborhoods, adding landmark downtown institutions, expanding its girth, generating its geographical, demographical, philosophical, and architectural personality. Its meaning, in other words. Its big shoulders. Then, in the second half of the century, as these places slid into decline, so did that meaning, and all the logic of its previous trajectory.

Akron, in 2010, had to face that its population had recoiled, for the first time, all the way back to its 1910 level. Population-wise, a city built on the auto industry was literally back to the horse-and-carriage days.

What that means on a personal level is that I have spent my whole life watching people leave, such that it has become my sad-sack cartoon catchphrase. For anyone who has committed his or her self to a place like this, that becomes a defining characteristic, perhaps *the* defining characteristic. That we have stayed when it seems as if everyone else has left.

At some point, it forces the hardest question.

Why?

My friends Michael and Chuck and I used to hang out regularly at a terrible bar I'll call the Withering Frog, whose business model was selling overpriced drinks in a blandly decorated room to a clientele that pushed dollar bills into a jukebox with no good songs except maybe Creedence's "Fortunate Son." They did serve a decent hamburger, but I'm hesitant to add that fact because in Middle America this can only serve as a backhanded compliment. It's kind of hard to mess up Angus in the heartland. On weekends, the Frog was packed with Dave Matthews fans, who, interestingly, seemed to thrive in a bland place with insufferable music. Week-nights, we had it mostly to ourselves.

The only reason we went there is because Chuck possesses a strong personality and insisted this be our regular gathering place because it was about fifty yards from the front door of his apartment.

"What are the three most important qualities in a bar?" he was fond of asking cheekily. "Location, location, location."

The only time I ever appreciated this was one night when I had to carry him home.

So for a few years, we were established "regulars," in the sense that our waitresses vaguely recognized us and we had no other options within Chuck's draconian parameters. The place being rather desolate on a random Tuesday night, our server would sometimes bring us a round of shots, including one for herself, and join us for a few minutes of conversation. (Those drinks always showed up on the bill later. It really was a terrible bar.)

So this went on for a few years until Michael one night announced that he was moving to Boston for graduate school. This was certainly a good move for him, forward and upward, and we celebrated his departure at the Withering Frog, toasting his future and wishing him Godspeed.

With Michael gone, Chuck and I held auditions for his replacement. This is neither a metaphor nor an exaggeration. We scheduled a series of tryouts among our acquaintances whose alcohol tolerance and trivia capacity suggested potential. The competition was robust. The winner was our friend Greg, who proved a brilliant replacement. Where Michael had provided a dry wit and deep knowledge of sports statistics, Greg tended to get loud and passionate when drunk and also possessed a remarkable knowledge of the funeral industry, adding an entirely new aural and material dynamic to the gatherings.

Then after a year or so, Greg announced that he was taking a job in Cincinnati. So once again we gathered at the Frog, toasted our farewells, and as the evening dwindled, Chuck and I scanned the holdouts, wondering who would be the next point of this little triangle. Another round of interviews and auditions. The winner was our friend Eric, who at this point was like the drummer in Spinal Tap. Eric was yet another excellent choice, brimming with energy and personality and an impressive expertise on early Killing Joke minutiae.

So we cruised along, not missing a beat, until the night Chuck announced that he was moving to New York City. Hawkeye Pierce, in other words, had gotten his transfer to Honolulu. We held Chuck's going-away party at the Withering Frog. He left town and I never set foot in that goddamn place again. It burned down a short time later.

Eric and I carried on in the manner of *AfterMASH*. It was a great friendship. Unlike Michael and Greg and Chuck, Eric was a local native who'd moved away for several years, then returned, so we shared a parochial bond, an understanding of place. Therefore, the day Eric announced he was taking a new job in Washington, DC, was pause not just for the usual melancholy and social adjustment, but for a sudden, jarring reassessment of my own self.

The old question—why do they keep leaving?—jumped on me like a knuckleball.

Why do I keep staying?

The whole idea of a "best friend" is borderline silly when you're a middle-aged husband and father in Ohio, a state that, according to the voting record, tends to view with suspicion any sort of same-sex partnership, bowling leagues notwithstanding. And the parsing of the idea seems even sillier.

Even so, other than my wife, I've always had roughly two official best friends—one who tends to be the person I most often hang out with socially (see above), and the other who is John Puglia. Throughout all of this change and departure and disillusion and evolution, he has always been here as coconspirator and reinforcement and reminder. We went through college and early postcollege sharing a fascination for the faded circumstances and the grit of our landscape, running around in it as if it were ours alone, which mostly it was. We were groomsmen in one another's weddings, bought old houses and became fathers around the same time, and began our careers in parallel fashion, both joining deeply rooted local institutions with some sort of national presence. John worked his way up through the ranks of Roadway Express, which was established in Akron in 1930 to transport tires manufactured here and quickly became a pioneer in freight trucking. He was director of corporate communications—the kind of fancy job at a Fortune 500 company that people from other parts of the world often forget exists even now in cities like ours. Or that they simply assume does not exist here. John helped guide the company through a 2003 merger with the Yellow Corporation, with corporate power transferring to the new parent, YRC, in Overland Park, Kansas. Meanwhile, I got a job at the *Akron Beacon Journal*, which, helmed for decades by Pulitzer Prize–winning newspaper icon John S. Knight, was the cornerstone of the powerful Knight Ridder newspaper chain and had a strong national reputation, even as the corporation was overtaken by the Ridder family and the headquarters moved to the Silicon Valley at the height of that region's fashionable opulence.

Although both John and I had ambition and both of us had good opportunities elsewhere, at some point, we felt as if we'd beaten the system, having found stability and opportunity and happiness in our hometown. Our lives had greater meaning here. Many of our friends who'd departed had landed in big cities perceived to have more of an upside. Bigger skyscrapers, more immediate power, prestigious national profiles. Chicago, New York, Seattle. These places also had stress levels and costs of living and degrees of alienation two or three or four times that of Akron. Here, rush hour is about ten minutes and graceful old houses in stable neighborhoods can be had for less than $100,000. Our extended families were nearby, and the easier lifestyle allowed us to pursue personal projects that made us happy. The Millworks, for instance.

By the time I felt like a grown-up, I had a solid and admittedly simple answer for the question of why I'd stayed in my hometown:

All my stuff is here.

A confession: I sometimes resent people who move back.

I don't resent that they moved back. That would be entirely hypocritical. My resentment is only maybe 22 percent hypocritical. What I resent is when they move back and presume to understand. There's my hypocrisy: I want to be understood. But I also harbor the old *Shaft*-esque one-liner: "It's a Rust Belt thing. You wouldn't understand." Because really—if my having never left doesn't at least provide me with some version of authority, then what have I got?

I sat on a radio panel one time with a man who'd done just that, gone off and lived much of his life in New York City, then returned to his hometown of Cleveland, and he wanted to tell the world that we in Ohio had just as much going for us as the Manhattanites among whose number he had until recently counted himself. He was telling us—his fellow panelists and whoever was listening—about all these local treasures as though we needed to be reminded of our worth, or perhaps that we had not done a proper job of calculating and projecting it. The Cleveland Orchestra. A local jazz club. A Great Lake. And it's not so much that he was condescending (though he *was* condescending). It's that he wasn't giving us credit for our least-appreciated, yet perhaps most important, asset: the ownership of loss.

We're not Manhattan. But for some reason this comes up time and time again, this suggestion that our worth can only be measured upward. Cleveland has been called the Paris of the Rust Belt. Pittsburgh has been called the Paris of Appalachia. Detroit's been called the Paris of the Midwest. Cincinnati, for God's sake, has been called the Paris of America. But what about living in the Akron of Ohio? What about saying it's my favorite city, and not because it compares favorably to other cities—places I also love—but because it doesn't.

The place I love is a three-legged dog. Everyone who's ever loved a three-legged dog knows you love that dog more than one with a handsome pedigree. Because it needs you more. And that's what true love is: the warmth of being needed.

Wait. That sounds like a redemptive ending.

There will not be a redemptive ending. Redemptive endings are easy, and we're not wired that way.

In that same radio conversation, another panelist declared that it was time to hang up the tired old term Rust Belt and find something new, something more hopeful and uplifting. A lot of people in these parts are partial to the term North Coast, referring to our location on Lake Erie. Soon the conversation developed into a debate about whether Cleveland would be the literal north coast of Erie, or if that would be Canada on the other side, the whole thing devolving into an Escher-like debate about spatial perspective. This is how self-conscious we are, how wired we are to second-guess, how prone we are to craft a preemptive defense. (For a long time, remember, Cleveland was called the Mistake on the Lake. It's understandable.)

We need to be the Rust Belt. We've paid so dearly for that designation that we deserve to have it as our own and to allow it to represent the fullness of its story. It's our blues.

In 2008 the Rust Belt came into its power.

It didn't recover, or rather didn't reach some magic level of recovery. Rather, it matured in its perspective as it continued to struggle back. We had endured this way for a quarter century, long enough to have gained insight and a bigger-picture view: that resiliency and persistence and an instinct for reinvention in the face of ongoing hardship offer better lessons than an ultimate redemption.

The presidential election that year focused on the economy, on the housing crisis, on the loss of manufacturing, on the auto industry plight, on the potential weakening of the American Dream. Our region had been working through these realities for a generation, had taken ownership of them, and was evolving from them in a realistic way.

For the first time in a long time, we in the Industrial Belt could step forward and offer ourselves as a useful example, as experts on something, as the very best.

Hard times?

We are the Paris of Hard Times.

I spent that year reporting on the election again, this time with a more immediate focus. My colleague David Knox at the *Akron Beacon Journal* had conducted groundbreaking research to show that we were living in the first American generation in which parents could not statistically expect their children to do better than they had. The defining tenet of the American Dream was endangered. His research was well ahead of the mainstream, preceding the widespread perception of a deep-in-the-culture financial crisis by nearly a year.

The newspaper conducted focus groups, and night after night I listened to tale after tale of a profound anxiety—of debt and uncertainty and diminished expectations. There was hope too, but of a ragged and stubborn sort. I wrote about people in bankruptcy and people who'd lost once-secure manufacturing jobs and people who worried they'd never be able to retire and people burdened with student-loan debt. I stood in a garage with a mother holding back tears as her just-graduated son backed a loaded-down midsize economy car out of the driveway and onto the street where he'd grown up, a street called Bittersweet Lane. This was the last of her three children, her last child to leave, on his way to New York City to test his possibility.

I picked up a ringing telephone two weeks later to learn that her husband had just been laid off, followed by the hardest words of the contemporary American middle class:

"Now what?"

I conducted this work in a newsroom that was itself living those very concerns. The *Beacon Journal* had, like all American newspapers in the past dozen years, suffered deeply declining circulation and revenues and severe cutbacks in personnel and resources. A 2012 report identified the newspaper industry as having suffered the worst decline of any American industry between 2007 and 2011. My own newsroom had been hit with the first layoffs in its history in 2001, when the staff was cut via pink slips and buyouts.

In 2006, Knight Ridder was purchased by the McClatchy newspaper chain, which immediately jettisoned the twelve lowest-performing newspapers. We were one of them. I've never been in a more anxious workplace.

Waiting to find out who'd buy us, the staff in the old newspaper offices heaved with uncertainty and worry. Within a couple of months, the company was purchased by a Canadian publisher, David Black, who, in a memo to the staff, said there would be no layoffs. Almost immediately upon taking ownership, he eliminated 25 percent of the news staff.

When I had joined the paper twelve years before, the newsroom employed around 200 people. When Black took over, the paper was at about 160. After his first round of staff cuts, it was down to about 120.

So maybe it's not such a surprise that David Knox was able to foresee the coming recession. Reporting on the plight of the middle class from within the Akron newsroom that year was kind of like studying whale depopulation from aboard a sinking ship.

All year, I visited with and wrote about people whose lives reflected the truths of the postindustrial Midwest. It wasn't an entirely bleak story. It wasn't as simple as campaign narratives would suggest. Some of the people who'd suffered most had reinvented themselves in remarkable and uplifting ways. Many people—probably most—were carrying on, concerned, but resolute. Most of us felt that we were doing our best within a system that felt dangerous, volatile, strained by conditions that had been maturing over the past generation—the very generation into which I'd been born.

And so, as the election season picked up pace in the fall and the economy was quickly rising to the forefront as the dominant American concern, word spread around the newspaper that another round of staff cuts was coming. The owner would be offering buyouts. This might be the last chance for any of us to get out on our own terms.

I decided to leave.

Here's a Paris story.

Or close enough, anyway. To my parochial mind, any story about France may as well be a Paris story.

On the afternoon of September 25, 2009, John Puglia was enjoying one of the best days of his life, strolling with his girl-friend through a plaza in Vernon, France. They'd just returned by bicycle from a visit to Monet's home and garden and had shared a bottle of wine and a picnic lunch from a local shop. John's cell phone rang.

It was human resources. They were turning off his phone. The one he was holding to his ear. He was not to return to the office. His desk would be cleared and his belongings would be boxed and delivered to his home. After sixteen years with the trucking company, he was being terminated. The company had lost hundreds of millions of dollars that year and had already laid off thousands of workers and slashed pay and benefits within the remaining work-force. The landmark Akron headquarters had been dwindling since the 2003 merger, and YRC was about to put the building up for sale.

That was the story of that year. Reduction upon reduction. People who managed to keep their jobs were loaded up with the duties of their departed colleagues and knew better than to complain about it. "Doing more with less" became the corporate mantra not just in the Rust Belt, but across the country.

Akron is a city where, twenty years before, "keeping your job" meant being retained at the factory just long enough to shut it down, and having no choice but to do that work, knowing there might not be anything beyond.

Some of the country was stunned in 2008; we were well acquainted with the feeling.

I don't know if I'd call that vindication, but in these parts we're not too well acquainted with vindication.

I began teaching at the University of Akron. John, after his layoff, made looking for a job his full-time job. We sat at my dining room table and brainstormed, made lists, worked on his résumé. John kept going with freelance work, and after three months he found a place where maybe he'd belonged all along, a job as creative director at a marketing agency in a historic nineteenth-century building that had been a warehouse in the canal era, and a storage building for Model T's, and a horse stable. We'd known it as one of those stubborn, faceless buildings of our old downtown, and now it was rejuvenated as the kind of place we'd always imagined in the void.

PRETTY VACANT

My wife is petite, healthy and strong—enough to have birthed two babies and survived a childhood home with six siblings and one bathroom, and to have hammered out a life with a frequently illogical husband. She is quite beautiful, exercises regularly, eats right, has all her teeth and a lot of nice dresses. The phrase *brick hauler* is not the first that comes to mind.

Except for one thing.

So. There we were. An overnight getaway. A hot summer afternoon at the foot of Mount Washington, next to a chain-link fence separating us from the CSX tracks and the Monongahela River and the stunning skyline of Pittsburgh beyond, her in a polka-dotted sundress, scanning the ground diligently as I did so expertly.

"There's one," she said, pointing next to a clutch of weeds a little ways up the hillside.

"Nope," I said. "That's a building brick."

"How can you tell?"

"I can tell."

Full disclosure: this was our wedding anniversary.

We continued along the edge of the road. There—there's one. No. Wait. Almost, but missing a corner. There—another, sticking up through the dirt, but—no, uh-uh, the face is crumbling. A half brick. Another half brick. Three-quarters of a brick. And then, a little way up the rise, a promising shape. I scaled the rubble and rolled it over with my foot. A keeper.

A light terra-cotta paver, more tan than red, a street brick worn at the corners, nine inches by three and three-quarters, eight pounds, stamped in block letters:

PENNA
CLAY Co.

I hauled it down the hillside and set it near her sandaled feet. I'd said I only wanted one, but now that the search had begun and borne fruit, I was hungry for another. Blood in the water, etc. A little farther along, I found an exceptional one, flat on top, nice rounding at the edges. And then a bonus surprise, the broken half of a flat fire brick, bearing the cryptic letters of the first half of its stamping: BENEZ—. And there, up the hillside, one more PENNA block, a gift for my father.

And that, I promised, would be it.

"Do you mind carrying one?" I said, offering her a paver while I gathered up the other three.

"I can take two," she sighed.

We made our way back to the car.

It is in many ways an unfortunate term: Ruin Porn. It has taken hold in recent years, somewhere in the same lexical parking lot as Rust Belt and industrial rock and brownfield and brain drain. Ruin Porn is applied mainly to photography of abandoned, decaying urban spaces and has especially been focused on the postindustrial regions of the Midwest and Appalachia and on toward the East Coast, with urban explorers—ranging from amateur point-and-shooters to high-profile artists—trespassing in empty buildings and distressed neighborhoods, documenting what others have ignored.

The art of Camilo José Vergara, Matthew Christopher, Sean Posey, Andrew Moore, Yves Marchand, and Romain Meffre typifies this style, and although their approaches and philosophies vary greatly, a consistent thread of criticism of exploitation dogs them, some deserved, some not. Their work unfolds inside collapsed libraries where trees have taken root in rotting texts. And in vacant factories, floors strewn with trash, paint on the brick walls curling into psychedelic hieroglyphs of neglect. And around foreclosed homes succumbing to mold and rot. And along polluted rivers strung with run-down industrial strips. And in abandoned theaters and churches and transit stations, places dripping with the tension between opulence and decadence.

Here's one I'm looking at right now, by the photographer Andrew Moore, of a collapsing nursing home on Seven Mile Road, a closely framed image of a room with broken ceiling tiles littering the floor, one wall blasted open, another wall on which someone has spray-painted a message that in any other context would seem melodramatic: GOD HAS LEFT DETROIT.

Moore's work was the subject of a major exhibition, *Detroit Disassembled,* curated by the Akron Art Museum in 2010. The photographs in that collection are huge, several feet across, and hyperreal, and entirely familiar to those of us who exist in cities that continue to struggle back up from a collapse.

Here's another: an empty office at the former Ford Motor Company headquarters, the rich floor-to-ceiling wood paneling mottled with water damage, the green carpet distorted into a weird rotten grid. (I once explored an eerily similar office at the former General Tire headquarters, a blastedly cold, profoundly empty interior decorated with stained glass of the founding-family crest.)

And another: the ornate ballroom of the Lee Plaza Hotel, where the paint on the arched ceilings and the broad walls is alligatored, flaked, and crumbling, the vast expanse of center space anchored by a collapsed grand piano. (I made a table out of slabs of marble salvaged from the floor of Akron's historic, abandoned Portage Hotel just before it was demolished.)

And another: the James Scott Mansion, a stone castle with a turret and grand arched entrance, its windows all smashed out, walls overtaken by ivy. (I live in a gracious Tudor home with six fireplaces, stained-glass windows, servants' quarters, and a billiards room, purchased on the verge of condemnation from underneath a stack of health-department orders, a house that was infested with wildlife, with no working plumbing, no safe electricity, overwhelmed with decay.)

I've always felt inspired by such places and never thought about feeling any other way.

One night, exploring downtown in the moonlight when I was still in college, I found an old metal colander in the weeds near the canal and picked it up and carried it with me. I had no practical purpose for this. I don't recall being in need of a spaghetti strainer nor recognizing some resale value in this random kitchen implement. It was just the old scavenging instinct at work, a notion bred into my generation to catch things before they fall into irrelevance.

The *Detroit Disassembled* show was preceded by an exhibition of Lee Friedlander's *Factory Valleys* collection, those photos of Akron, Pittsburgh, Cleveland, and Canton in the early 1980s, and then by the photographs of Andrew Borowiec, distinguished professor of art at the University of Akron, who moved to the city in the crucial year of 1984 and has made the social-industrial landscape a main subject ever since.

The three exhibits placed in that context depict three distinct visions/versions of an unfolding story. Friedlander shows the last days of a highly evolved, once-thriving culture. Moore shows the highly evolved, thriving ruins.

Borowiec's work does something different. (Full disclosure: Andrew Borowiec is a friend, and I have written the introduction to one of his books.) The museum displayed photographs from two of his collections in separate galleries. The first set, from his *Along the Ohio* project, contained black-and-white images of mostly small-town and urban landscapes near the Ohio River, taken in the 1980s and '90s. The second was from his series *The New Heartland*, photographs from 2004 to 2009 depicting the suburban and rural residential and commercial development that has represented a next phase of Middle American evolution.

Which is to say that Friedlander and Moore offer the drama of a moment and Borowiec offers an ongoing narrative rumination. And there is the key difference. Borowiec maintains a continuing engagement with his environment, and an emotional connection to the conditions behind it, and regardless of whether that makes his art better, it provides an ethical transcendence, one particularly important in places like this, where the story is more often told by someone who has parachuted in, with return ticket at the ready.

The prevailing criticism of Ruin Porn is that such art is exploitive of someone else's pain, that it does nothing to address solutions, that it invites slumming aesthetes, that it rarely reflects people interacting with these usually very public spaces, that it sensationalizes, that it isolates the worst of a community from the context of the bigger and far more complex socioeconomic picture.

Moore offered a preemption by including text panels alongside some of his *Detroit Disassembled* images, offering wider context to the immediate scene, often injecting a tone of hope and perseverance. Friedlander's series, as arranged in the book *Factory Valleys*, evolves from desolate urbanscapes to portraits of workers in their environment, indicating a desire to connect the drama of the visual moment to the real lives it contains.

Yet, despite these attempts, I find a recurring frustration, an old defensiveness, rising in my response. In 2009, the *New York Times Magazine* ran a cover piece by Alex Kotlowitz titled "All Boarded Up," about the housing foreclosure crisis, visiting a Cleveland neighborhood where a third of the houses were vacant, in a city where an estimated one in every thirteen homes was in foreclosure. The story was deeply reported, sensitive to its subjects, well written, apparently accurate, and yet I found myself bristling at its myopia.

What about what's happening a mile away? What about the suburbs? What about the highway between the cities, onion layers of nuance unfolding mile by mile? What about the urban neighborhoods that are actively working toward their own vitality? What about the patchwork of these cities, the way the social personality often changes radically from one block to the next? (My wife and I have owned two houses, both in the same middle-class neighborhood, a half mile apart. Our current home is in a solid, stable, relatively safe city block. Our previous home was next door to a Section 8 crack house. How to tell that story simply?)

So, even in the work of Friedlander, which I find historically essential, and the work of Moore, which I find visually arresting, and in the work of Kotlowitz, which I find journalistically sound, I have the old, impossible-to-shake, involuntary response.

He's not one of us.

This is mine.

This is who I am.

I want to be the one to define it.

Friedlander and Moore came from their studios in New York to do their work. Kotlowitz came from suburban Chicago. They all went back home when they were done.

So my struggle is not so much with them or their work, but with my own internal paradox, which is just a fancy term for my own hypocrisy, a hypocrisy that is at least a minor plague among my people—I don't want them to interpret me, *even if they get it exactly right.*

In regular excursions of my childhood, I rode shotgun with my father in one of his company's tin-can surveying trucks or in his shit-brown Impala station wagon, off to collect what he was prone to describe, deliciously, as a "mother lode." I came to know the very smell of approaching clay and stone in the shimmer of summer heat, and the ceremonious arrival, taking stock, then clawing through piles of unearthed street brick, or the rubble of a demolition site or the holding yard of a highway-construction contractor. Hot, dusty afternoons, I learned the heft of a paver, the century-old interlocking street bricks he craved for his readaptations in walkways and patios. I learned, very young, the qualities of age, of wreckage, of wear, of patina. These were not so much described to me as they were inscribed on me.

I learned how to read the faces of the bricks, and the stories they told—BESSEMER BLOCK and BIG FOUR and AKRON BLOCK and HARRIS ZANESVILLE. Sometimes the letters were so worn that we couldn't make out the words, and so the stories deepened, mysteries that drew us to crayon rubbings or just accepting the unknowable nature of some things.

Sometimes the stampings were ornate. We once found a whole pile shot through with commemorative bricks from the 1893 Chicago world's fair, decorated with an elaborate depiction of Columbus's discovery of America, commemorating the previous year's four-hundredth anniversary of the event, which provided the fair's theme. When I rebuilt my front stoop, I incorporated rows of these lighter-colored bricks into the pattern. (I recently looked the World's Fair paver up on Google and found an eBay listing for one with the current price of $10.49. Even though I knew these bricks are rare, this was the first time the notion of their monetary value ever occurred to me. Partly because I'd never sell one, and partly because I've never paid for one.)

Such intrigue was more the exception than the rule. The stampings generally were simple, pragmatic, and pointedly regional: CLEVELAND BLOCK; CANTON METROPOLITAN.

My dad was a connoisseur of ruins. He befriended the guy who had the contract to demolish buildings for the city, and so these excursions grew into elaborate, exotic outings, sometimes requiring whole weekends and skid loaders. When I was in my early twenties, my dad asked me if I could round up half a dozen friends because he'd scored scavenging rights to the foundation of a demolished barn and had bartered to borrow a flatbed truck for a Sunday. So I showed up with a carload of sleepy-eyed, hungover, self-taught musicians and an itinerant stand-up comic, the lot of them dressed in canvas sneakers and Hüsker Dü T-shirts and jelly bracelets, not altogether prepared for this sort of work, lured chiefly by the promise of twenty-five bucks apiece. (My father, fully expecting such a scenario, had brought along a bucket full of work gloves.)

Down the hillside behind the barn site, I found a junked washing machine, scrambled down to it, pulled off the chunky, silver plastic knobs and instantly recognized the size and shape of the control stems. Sure enough, when I got home that night and tried them on the volume and tone controls of my Fender Mustang, they fit perfectly, and I played it that way for years, looking as if I were adjusting for temperature and rinse cycle.

Was I drawn to these things because I was following my father's instincts? Did their elemental nature appeal to me naturally as a child, a real-life version of LEGOS? Was it because of the male appetite for destruction? Was it because of the architecture of my place? Would I have the same attraction if I'd grown up in, you know, Phoenix, where the bricks are all new and synthetic?

I can't say for sure. What I do know is that for as long as I can remember, I have been far more attracted in every way to things that are worn and used than to clean, new things. I find reclaimed bricks superior to new in every way, in their quality of craft, their appearance, their weight. And I find them even more desirable in dumped piles, or lying at random near the bottom of their tumbled walls, or peeking up from the hard dirt, leached from a Pittsburgh hillside. I like them when they're hard to get.

Recognizing the value of forgotten and broken things seems, at least in my part of the country, to be the story of America in the twenty-first century. The 1900s were all about making things. The new millennium has been all about remaking things.

My father sits now most summer afternoons in a little porch he built next to his garage. To visit him there, I first pass a hand-built stone column into which he set the sculpted-in-the-round face of a girl, saved from the demolition of a local public school. Then, underfoot, a precious lifelong collection, laid into a brick path.

FULTONHAM
STEEL PAVER
NEWBURGH
IRON ROCK
PORTER
20th CENTURY

And now, off to the side, PENNA, awaiting its place.

UNREAL ESTATES

I used to know these places from their insides out. I knew them before their synthetic skins were applied and the prefabricated bluegrass was rolled between driveways and before the plastic mullions were pressed onto the safety glass to give the illusion of panes. I knew them before their gardens were delivered in plastic buckets, their varnish sprayed on like a news anchor's Aqua Net. I worked at residential construction sites in college doing shit work with a lot of that time spent not doing anything, just exploring, noodling around the lives of people who were spending fantastic amounts of money—the kind measured in percentages of a million—for houses made of extruded foam and synthesized brick and bar-code-stamped green lumber from force-fed firs.

I had a whole ring of keys, like a watchman. I went from house to house, often in the off-hours, at twilight and dawn, usually tending to the tedium: the add-ons, the do-overs, the cleanups after the big crews had packed up their caravans and moved on to the next little castle. I snooped through the half-unpacked lives, the soft-core pornography and the unpaid bills and the ceramic Precious Moments. In the shadowy musk of fresh-laid carpet, I stared at unhung portraits of people who didn't match the tired-looking, well-dressed new-owners-but-not-yet-occupiers who stopped in on the fly to see how much longer it would be until they could call this home. Their Bimmers idled on the unsealed concrete, impatient. I stole a beer or two from their refrigerators—always, *always* Miller Lite—and peered into the shadows of a lifestyle that I, more green than the studs behind the Sheetrock, could only decipher as foreign, hard to plumb.

These people had money. They had a lot of money. And there were a lot of them. Whole new developments full. There's this impression that when the industrial collapse happened, it devastated entire regions of the country. But it was much more nuanced than that. Some demographics (for lack of a more human word) were crushed, yes—driven away, or down into a lower standard of living. Yet others thrived. And some weren't much affected one way or the other.

(Conversely, I specifically remember cutting brush on one of those building lots the afternoon of October 19, 1987, listening to radio news of the stock market crash that would label that day Black Monday, and wondering how it would affect this group of people who seemed so intertwined with high finance. And also wondering if I, with a few hundred dollars to my name, had any reason to be personally concerned.)

Most of the houses I worked on were in a wealthy suburban township called Bath, a place that had always been wealthy, and suburban, and township-ish. There's probably a version of this place in the outer ring of every industrial center in America, the civic equivalent of the restaurant most people would only go to for prom or a landmark anniversary, but also has a small, rarefied core of regulars.

The developer I worked for was once quoted in the local newspaper about his emphasis on building stately homes on large, gracious plots of land.

"We want to keep Bath, *Bath*," he said, implying a semantic exclusivity: the proper noun was its own modifier.

So I was given intimate insight into the distinctions of what I would call the wealthy working class. I saw that, for whatever opportunities and advantages they had, they also did work hard, leaving early in the morning and getting home late in the day, and often traveling long distances, often under high stress, to the work that would continue to provide the lifestyle they had achieved.

By this comparison, I was given insight into the distinctions of my own life as a student at the local public university, a son of the slightly-upper-middle working class. My mom was a grade-school teacher and my dad was an engineer. With their help and the money I saved from my summer jobs, I made it through college without loans. I recognize now that, as I finished my university courses in 1990, I was among the last Americans for whom college was affordable in this way. The cost of a year's tuition at my alma mater, the University of Akron, has nearly quadrupled since then.

The conspicuousness of the lifestyle these homes represented allowed me to wonder, as I began planning my own life, what I wanted from it. And it allowed me, as I returned to a different kind of home, an old place, built in a much different way, to wonder what it meant. My parents' house, where I lived, was constructed in the 1930s, during the boom years of the automobile era, which was when the Rubber City matured, civically and architecturally. The house took on the physical demeanor it maintains, albeit under much different conditions, to this day. My dad was constantly working on our house, and so I came to understand tangibly how it was built: the weight of a well-forged hinge, the thickness of a prewar baseboard, the density of an old stud, the tenacity of plaster. These were standard materials in their day. They represented the way Americans did things then, the way we thought things ought to be done.

* * *

These places where I worked were the best that money could buy. I knew the carpenters and plumbers and electricians and roofers. I knew the men who installed the foam-filled garage doors and the ones who screwed on the drywall and the ones who glued down the veneers. They were craftsmen, the best at their trades, true to the American Rustic. (Some of them were gypsies, plying their skills cross-country, rooming in Days Inns, jobbing from subdivision to subdivision, free as a taxpayer can be in the modern age.) They were earnest and hardworking and took genuine pride in the process and the product. No question about that. So too were the people who commissioned these places: themselves earnest and hardworking, though I never understood what they did exactly— something to do with annuities and trusts. They always had file boxes of that inscrutable green-and-white-striped paper with the perforated edges, and I could reckon all day and never get to the bottom of it. But, yes, I recognized that they viewed the newness of these houses as a marker of personal and cultural achievement. They seemed to recognize the verb roots of *development* and *housing* as a gerund. Everything in the active tense, the desperate yearning of progress.

But I began to understand, from the inside out, that these places had a falseness, that they were inorganic, that they would not age gracefully, that the advanced chemistry of their paint would simply chalk and fade, would never alligator into the wizened shell of old clapboards. I knew that their aluminum fencework would never rust, that posts made of advanced metals would simply stick up there, simple-headed, never gaining the mantle of oxidation. Their shells were so slick. There was nothing for patina to cling to. There would never be anything wrong with them that a good power washing couldn't fix.

And I came to see that they couldn't last. That they wouldn't stand up to the onslaughts of nature, the advances of age. The old farmland and woods from which these new parcels arose extended from what once was a country highway, itself now lined with new construction, a fast-growing commercial strip of boxes and prefabrication. All of it overtaken by a construction that seemed oblivious of the past and ignorant of the future, implying a cynical fabrication of disposable income.

Yet I also knew that this was the best America had to offer. These were the best carpenters and masons, and these were the best materials currently being produced, and these were the best buyers, and that this was the best our upwardly mobile imagination could fashion.

The American century was ending. We had built it ourselves.

The state of Ohio is shaped like a heart. The reason it is shaped this way is because of the south-and-east-border-defining Ohio River and the Great Lake to the north—the unbuilt landscape. On a hill near the developments described above, I can stand during a rainstorm and watch the water drain in two directions: north, to Lake Erie, and south, to the Ohio River. This is the watershed. It goes right through the heart of the heart-shaped state. There seems to be something decisive about that, comfortingly simple. It is either this way, or that. We call it the Ohio Divide.

Ohio, and places like it, are most often viewed from the outside as simple in this way, as the part of the country where the contents of the pot actually melted into some sort of consistent American stew that can be sampled whenever there's a need to know the true flavor.

Few people ever ask what we think about anything until they have some need, and then they come here for answers, to observe Middle Americans in the wild. Except the "wild" has been domesticated into these imitation neighborhoods and little commercial blocks that look like minitowns of full-grown Department 56 collectibles. This fabrication is supposed to represent the real America.

Here we are, nestled alongside the Breadbasket, established as the soft potbelly above the Bible Belt. But that notion of settlement, of docility, of completion, belies the strong influence of our borders and our sense of "beyond." The Ohio River, the thing that defines our eastern and southern boundary, feeds right into the mighty Mississippi, urging us toward our wild American theme. The northern border is the coastline of a Great Lake, a vista to the vast beyond.

Over several years, inspired by the contentious presidential election of 2004 in which Ohio (as always) played a pivotal role, my friend Andrew Borowiec traveled the state, taking photographs of this newly built landscape, of the false fronts and synthetic veneers and factory-grown landscaping. He compiled them into a collection called *The New Heartland*. The pictures contain no people, just the environments, deeply, often wryly considered.

The wide perspective of Borowiec's photographs compels me to look toward their farther reaches, to see past the façades, to wonder about the possibilities, and whether we've built them right out of the picture. There, at the far edge of one image, is a terrible, stunning pun: The "beyond" follows "Bed Bath &." The border is a Borders.

In another, a basketball hoop at the end of a lane between two new houses suggests completion, the end of exploration, that this place has satisfied some formula of the American Dream. Yet, in the near distance is a dense forest—a border and a beyond—but the photograph suggests that the child who practices foul shots at that basket would never think to venture into the woods.

A new swimming pool intrudes upon the bank of the Ohio River as though to nudge it out to pasture. Except there's no pasture.

One of the ways I used to describe the heartland is to say that this is the place where we call things by what they used to be. In my own hometown, a university building occupies what once was one of the big downtown department stores. Students have taken to calling it Polsky, but I always correct them. "It's Polsky's," I say, invoking the actual name of the store, then trying to fill the space between.

But these newly built places often strive overtly to disconnect from the past, clear-cutting mature trees, straightening and widening country lanes, elbowing out homegrown retail. When they do aspire to a history, they fumble for a past that never existed here. Their subdivision street names suggest half-assed delusions of classical grandeur, Anglophilic fetish, nostalgia for those olde tymes when one could shop for Levi's in a Hobbit village. Nostalgia without pain.

Borowiec chose some for the titles of his pictures:

Gramercy Street.

Misty Lane.

Legacy Court.

The developers call their new malls "lifestyle centers," and they offer strange, new lands of imagination, in which we can window-shop blouses at a J.Jill that looks like a mosque or worship at a church with a Walmart attitude.

Every four years, the politically inquisitive come back to probe Ohio, a state that still calls itself the "heart of it all." They regard this as a place where they can test the nation's pulse. They come here because they think we're average. And we are, I suppose. As average as a watershed. Some of us have more, and some of us have less; some of us think this way, and some of us think that. If you add it all up and divide by two, you get something in the middle.

The question is, the middle of what?

ASCENT

I sit in the passenger seat, strapped neatly against the gray cloth upholstery. His little sister has spilled a cola sometime in the recent past and I can see the dried, dark amoeba of its aftermath between my knees. Whatever. It's just a car. I've never had a very good one.

He adjusts his seat carefully, unsure of the levers, scooting it back with his long legs until the planks of his feet are situated to the pedals. He juts the key into the ignition and clicks it forward. The tape deck immediately blares, full volume. He recoils. I reach over and turn it off.

"Sorry," I say. "My fault."

(Really, it's *The Very Best of Elvis Costello and the Attractions'* fault, but I'm trying to assume a mantle of responsibility here.)

He tilts his shaggy blond head slightly upward, reaches forward, and adjusts the mirror, clicks intently from *P* through *R* and *N* to *D* and eases onto the accelerator. We roll forward.

Fifteen years, six months, twenty-two days. I do not know how this has happened. I still cannot for the life of me calculate how he got from the clutch of my shoulder to this—my driver—and how I got from all my years of wondering to here.

The question occurs from time to time whether my own father ever wondered such things, if maybe from across the room he looked at me and thought, *My Lord, what in the hell is that?*

Bewilderment has served me pretty well as a father. I seem to be able to teach better when I admit I don't know the answer than when I pretend I do, and that's good because I'm kind of an expert at not knowing the answer. Thank God my children can learn from my mistakes because sometimes it seems as if that's all I have. But that gimmick only goes so far—especially when you realize your twelve-year-old daughter has become even better with irony than you—and lately I've been thinking harder about what I do understand and what I do have to teach them. I've realized that almost all of it comes from what I know about myself, and almost all of *that* comes from what I know about my place—my home, its nature, its people. The forces that have shaped my psychic geology.

He asks me if it's safe to turn out of the driveway, and I tell him he's going to have to figure out that for himself, but not to worry, that I will scream in holy terror if he's wrong. So he looks again, this way, that way, this way once more, exhales, and makes the turn.

We ease from the road that follows the old Indian trail and turn left onto Market Street, the city's main road, the same path I have used for my whole life. We aren't really going anywhere. This is just practice, a way for him to start learning, to get comfortable. I know I'm supposed to be uptight, nervous, to be stamping against an imaginary brake pedal, but I don't find that in me. If I have anxiety, it's that my government is okay with me as the supervising adult.

We head east, under the pink-gold cast of an arriving winter dusk. The setting sun sometimes creates a sort of hyperillusion when you drive this route. Akron still doesn't have much of a skyline, and its shape can be gathered from only a couple of vantage points. But here, beginning down the hill this way from the city's highest point, you can see downtown in a way that seems compressed and also, in this early twilight, gilded, a glaze tilting across the old brick and new glass of the art museum, the Goodyear clock tower off in the far distance, the spires of Trinity Lutheran spiking through the center, the hospital building where the fancy, old hotel once stood, and occasionally, on a good day, the blimp up above. Sometimes it looks like a place I've never seen before.

We pass my old high school, which was John's high school, which was the first school where my wife taught, which was LeBron James's high school, which is now my son's high school, this mysterious young man who communicates best with a shy, crooked smile. I tell him to take a right, and he pauses, uncertain, glancing to me for guidance.

Right there, I say, pointing to the opening beyond a dark stone wall. Because, I realize now, we *are* going somewhere. We are going to Cadillac Hill, an oddly truncated stump of unnegotiable road that has no meaning or context unless someone is along to explain it, someone who's been here before.

Cadillac Hill rises up between some diced-up rental houses overlooking the old cemetery, the one where all the mustachioed colonels and the fancy philanthropists and the inventors and the industrial captains are buried, just beyond the house where Thomas Edison was married. It's in what the night-shift cops call a "known drug area," which is to say that a slowing-down car is likely to draw the attention of law enforcement. But I've never known anyone who slowed down on Cadillac Hill. That's not the point.

Nicknamed for its proximity to the city's only Cadillac dealership, the road is concocted of chunky nineteenth-century street bricks, which over the years have settled into a Seussian order, their joint lines softened into gentle sine waves, the edges tilted into a haphazard washboard. The rise is bafflingly steep—its grade exceeds 25 percent—and short. From its beginning down by the cemetery, to its peak, and back down to its other end, the road covers less than a city block. With its teeth-rattling surface and breathless rise-and-fall, it's more roller coaster than roadway.

At the bottom of the steepest end, the street's real name—Bates Hill—is carved into a granite obelisk that looks unmistakably like a grave marker.

Despite all of this, and because of all this, it has always been a destination, particularly for young men, one always taken at breakneck speed: a Springsteenian test of velocity, amplitude, aimlessness, anger, failure, freedom. It's the motoring equivalent of a tequila shot.

E-mail from my friend Chris, who works on the seventeenth floor of a downtown office building, received during an afternoon blizzard, February 12, 2008:

> *Happiness is . . . Watching a guy try again and again to drive his Geo Tracker up Cadillac Hill, only to watch him slow to a crawl, get sideways, and slide back down almost completely out of control. Only to loop around and try again. At least six times since we've been watching. The whole floor is standing at their windows, cheering for him.*

He realizes now that this is where we are headed. He's been here many times, but always sitting where I am now sitting, never as the driver. He rolls toward the foot of it, looking up the steep, jagged, timeworn brick.

I tell him to gun it, hard, as hard as he can, and we take it pretty fast, chattering up its rise, feeling it all the way through our bones, spirited by the jarring rush, and we hit the crest weightless, then slow into the curving decline, and at the bottom he looks to me for where to go next.

Do it again.

ACKNOWLEDGMENTS

I cannot overstate the support, commitment, and tenacity Daniel Greenberg has devoted to this book. He is a friend, a gentleman, and a true guardian.

Brant Rumble's brilliant enthusiasm and editorial harmony can best be summarized thus: He once e-mailed me on his day off (possibly from the zoo) upon random spontaneous realization that I may have misspelled smooth-jazz guitarist Lee Ritenour's name. And he was right.

Many and ongoing thanks as well to Nan Graham, Susan Moldow, Colin Harrison, Lauren Lavelle, Kara Watson, John Glynn, and everyone else at Scribner, and to everyone at Levine Greenberg Literary Agency.

The following people shared generously of their friendship, reading time, guidance, and/or bar tabs: Gina Giffels, John Puglia, Bob Ethington, Chuck Klosterman, Eric Nuzum, Michael Weinreb, Dave Rich, Andrew Borowiec, and Annie Murray. Thank you all.

Norma Hill, librarian at the *Akron Beacon Journal*, responded with deadeye accuracy to countless, often vaguely framed requests for information.

I owe enduring thanks to David Highfill, Lisa Gallagher, and Seale Ballenger at William Morrow for many, many good things. A hearty shout-out as well to my colleagues and students at the University of Akron and the Northeast Ohio Master of Fine Arts creative writing program, particularly Robert Pope, Eric Wasserman, and Mary Biddinger.

If faith is a belief in what you cannot see, then my family has granted me a remarkable gift, responding with patience, understanding, and encouragement as I disappear up a set of stairs and behind a closed door, day after day, year after year. Thank you Gina, Evan, and Lia for this, and all the rest.

Finally, and by no means least, my sincere thanks to the University of Akron Faculty Research Fellowship and the Cleveland Arts Prize for their generous support during the writing of this book.